The Ghosts of Tidewater
... and nearby environs

by L. B. Taylor Jr.

Photographs by the Author
Illustrations by Lisa Sullivan
Design by Howell Design, Inc.

ISBN 0-9628271-9-3

Contents

Acknowledgements

I was tremendously impressed by the enthusiasm, openness and friendly cooperation of the many, many people who helped me with this book. With hardly an exception, they told me their own stories and often encouraged me by leading me to others. With no exceptions, each source was genuinely interested not only in ghosts, but in having the tales compiled and published. Without such unselfish support, this book could not have been written. Following is a list of many of these contributors. If I have missed someone, I assure you it is purely unintentional, and probably caused by my own somewhat faulty memory. Nevertheless, I am deeply indebted to these gracious new friends.

Special thanks go to Charles Thomas Cayce, not only for granting an interview on his famous grandfather, but also for giving me leads on other area ghosts; and to the delightful Gerry McDowell, also from the Association for Research and Enlightenment. In the Williamsburg area, Shiela Lake, Dennis Watson, Dot Rascoe and Cathy Short were especially helpful, as were Robert Forest, Randy Rollins, Sr., and his son, Jack, in Poquoson. In Portsmouth, help came from Cathi Bunn, Bob Albertson, Gabrielle Bielenstein and George Gaffos; in Smithfield from Helen King and Mrs. H. D. DeShiell; in Gloucester from Peggy Licht and Ed Jenkins; in Mathews from Olivia Davis; and on the Eastern Shore from Floyd and Sam Nock.

Joe Law helped out at the Norfolk Naval Shipyard, as did Dennis Mroczkowski at Fort Monroe, Lisa Harrison at Evelynton Plantation, Bruce Johnson at West Point, Angie Reitzel and Whitney Elliot at the Pine Tree Inn in Virginia Beach, psychic investigator Tom Gulbranson, at several sites, and librarians throughout Tidewater.

I am particularly thankful to my friends Cindy Tatum and Ronnie Miles for their many helpful suggestions; to trance-medium Victoria Mauricio of Virginia Beach, who shared her astonishing story with me; to the lovely lady in Virginia Beach who must remain anonymous; to the effervescent Margaret Thompson who lived with a jealous ghost; and to Virginia

Beach psychic Mary Bowman and her equally gifted associate Kay Buchanan, who told me I had been a Confederate officer in the Civil War; to Marsha Smith, who led me to them; and to Odette Seekamp, who typed the manuscript; her husband Wesley, who proofread it and offered editorial suggestions; and to my cousins Jane Ward and Vance Shook, who, as always, lent their enthusiastic support.

And, finally, I dedicate this book to my new granddaughter, Emily Megan Willis.

Introduction

I had almost forgotten how much fun it is to write a book about ghost stories. After all, it had been eight years since I had done the research for my book, "The Ghosts of Williamsburg," and six years since I had visited haunted houses for "The Ghosts of Richmond."

It continues to amaze me as to how interested so many people are in ghosts. Since my first two area books, I have received hundreds of letters from "spectral fans" all over the country, many offering detailed reports of psychic experiences they have encountered. And even though I have never professed to be an expert on the subject, I have been asked to speak to dozens of clubs and organizations. (I have become a "Spooksperson"!) Shortly after the Richmond book came out I even hosted a Halloween tour of haunted houses in that city.

The research for this new book has also proved fascinating. It has led me from the brooding ruins of once-magnificent Rosewell in Gloucester County to the foreboding yet charismatic charm of the Great Dismal Swamp bordering Chesapeake and Suffolk; and from the darkened back alleys of historic Fort Monroe to the psychic havens of Virginia Beach.

Tidewater Virginia abounds in ghosts! And because so many different communities have been covered, there is, I believe, a richer assortment of stories in this book. Some of the houses and locations are well known; others are obscure. Some of the tales have been told and retold for generations. These I have tried to authenticate, freshen up, and to correct past inaccuracies. Many of the stories, however, are presented here for the first time anywhere.

There is everything from the more "traditional" ghosts and haunted houses to extraordinary instances of poltergeists and/or psychokinesis. There are ghost animals and ghost lights. There are "time warps" and "bleeding" stones. There is a ghost lover who comes back to sing on his sweetheart's tapes. There are "trance mediums" who have had visions which literally came to life. The time range runs from the 17th century to the present day. There is drama and tragedy, melancholy and comedy; a little bit of everything.

And everywhere, there has been the unbridled enthusiasm of the people involved; people who have experienced, and in some instances, influenced the phenomena. With one exception, the sincerity and voracity of these "witnesses" is, I firmly feel, genuine. The exception was a reported case of demonology some years ago in Portsmouth, which later proved to be a hoax. Some of the stories are, admittedly, folklorian in nature. But even here, as in the case of the Witch of Pungo, Grace Sherwood, there is ample documentation to substantiate the story.

As in my earlier books, I do not make a case for or against the believability of ghosts. I merely tell the stories that have been told to me. Readers may decide for themselves. And, as I have previously reported, the great majority of mysterious sights, sounds, smells and other "happenings" can be explained rationally. Old houses do creak and groan. Marsh gas and moonlight mixtures can conjure images and apparitions. Fertile imaginations can play tricks on the mind, as can alcohol or stimulants. Grief can also play a part at times. Such factors explain most "instances," but not all of them.

The remaining small percentage of inexplicable occurrences is included here. After researching hundreds of cases of reported phenomena related to ghosts, I have come to the personal belief that there *is* a realm of psychic phenomena about which we still know precious little. Some people are more sensitive to this psychic world than others. Despite many advances in this area in recent years, there is still much to be learned. Some day we may "break the code" and open the door to a greater understanding. To put it another way, as I have written before, in our technological age, ghostly manifestations may be hard to accept, but even the sternest skeptic should be aware that there is some sort of shadowy perimeter, as yet unreachable, that someday may be brought into sharper focus. How can anyone say for certain that it does not exist; that ghosts do not exist?

In this vein, I like to quote what expert Hans Holzer once wrote in one of his books: "Throughout the centuries, the skeptical, the scientific and the credulous have attempted to solve the mystery of ghosts and hauntings. There are theories, but no proofs, as to *why* things happen. But that the incidence of such happenings exceeds the laws of probability, and that their number establishes that there *is* something to investigate, is beyond dispute."

What are ghosts? I am often asked that. I still don't have an exact answer. The dictionary says a ghost is "a disembodied soul; the soul of a dead person believed to be an inhabitant of the unseen world or to appear to the living in bodily likeness." Holzer, one of the greatest authorities on ghosts, and the author of several books on the subject, says a ghost "appears to be a surviving emotional memory of someone who has died traumatically, and usually tragically, but is unaware of his (or her) death." Another version is that ghosts are visual (or otherwise) paranormal appearances, generally spontaneous, that suggest the real presence of someone distant or dead.

Dr. Karlis Osis, a psychologist with the highly respected American Society of Psychical Research in New York, has written that "if there is a real presence (to ghosts), then we have something from human personality which exists after death . . . It has been suggested that there is not a real human personality there, but something separate, a little fragment of some kind of energy hanging on. Here again, the question is, is there a real human being who died in an unfortunate circumstance, and somehow missed the bus, and stopped where he or she shouldn't be? They're stuck . . ."

Regardless of the definition and whether or not one believes, the real purpose of this book is not to take a stand for or against the existence of spirits, but rather, to entertain. The telling of ghost stories, a time-honored tradition that can be traced back thousands of years, is a dying art. The advent of modern technology, particularly television, has greatly diminished the once prominent oral tradition of spinning ghost stories. And I, for one, think this is sad. We are slowly losing what I consider a national treasure. That is one reason I have chosen to write this, my fourth book, on ghosts. Here, at least temporarily, will be preserved some of the rich legends and lore of our area's colorful past. Some of the chapters are preceded by appropriate quotes from the poetry of Edgar Allen Poe.

The question I have been most often asked is have I seen or experienced a ghost. The answer is still no. I did have what might be described as a close encounter, however. One blustery winter afternoon I was driving with a friend west on Route 5, the historic "back road" from Williamsburg to Richmond that is dotted with so many splendid plantation homes, some dating to the 1600s and 1700s. We stopped at Edgewood, a fine Victorian mansion run by the affable Dot Boulware. As the readers of my book, "The Ghosts of Williamsburg" know, Edgewood has its own ghost, "Miss Lizzie," who occasionally appears holding a candle in an upstairs window looking for her lost lover who never returned from the Civil War.

I got out of the car to deliver some books to Dot, who sells them in her gift shop. The front door was locked tight, and no one responded to my knocking and bell ringing. As I returned to my car, my friend said, "look, the door is open." I went back, and to my surprise, found it was indeed open. I went inside and called loudly, "anyone home?" No response. I then invited my friend to step inside to view the parlor, elegantly outfitted in period furniture.

My friend walked slowly through the room to its second entrance, and as she approached it, Dot Boulware opened the door to the basement and they met face to face. They scared the hell out of each other. We asked Dot if she had opened the front door. She said no. She hadn't heard us or anything else.

I like to think maybe it was Miss Lizzie!

There is just one last anecdote which I found both humorous and gratifying. In doing the research, I talked to one young lady in Gloucester who, in trying to be helpful, told me that her mother had a "marvelous" book all about ghosts and that if I could locate a copy in a library she was sure I would find everything I was looking for. She would ask her mother what the title was and get back to me. The next day she called and said the book was "The Ghosts of Richmond." The author was L. B. Taylor, Jr. We both had a hearty laugh over that when she realized who I was.

Writing this book has been fun. I met a lot of interesting and wonderful people, I visited a lot of fascinating places, and I heard a lot of compelling tales. I hope you will find them the same. Enjoy!

L. B. Taylor, Jr.

And travellers now, within that valley,
  Through the red-litten windows see
Vast forms, that move fantastically
  To a discordant melody,
While, like a ghastly rapid river,
  Through the pale door
A hideous throng rush out forever
  And laugh — but smile no more.

From "The Haunted Palace"
by Edgar Allan Poe

While I nodded, nearly
napping, suddenly there
came a tapping, As of some
one gently rapping, rapping
at my chamber door.

(*The Raven*)

The Rapping Friend of the Oystermen

t Fort Eustis, there is a small sheltered cove where the waters of Nell's Creek feed into the James River. Decades ago, before the government purchased the land surrounding this area, Nell's Creek was a haven for Tidewater oystermen. Daily, they would ply their time-honored trade amid the rich oyster beds of the James, nearby, and at night some would stay in the mouth of the creek from Monday night until Friday, when they would take their catch to market and head home.

Local lore has it that this particular creek was named after a young lady named Nell, who lived in the region, probably during the 19th century. No one seems to know her last name. What has been passed down is that she was a spirited, head-strong person who fell in love with a man described as a "straggler," and that her father strongly objected to such a union. In fact, that was putting it mildly. He allegedly told her that if she violated his wishes and married the man, he would kill her and bury her along with all his money.

To make a long story short, despite the warning, she ran off with her lover, and her father lived up to his threat. He killed her and buried her, supposedly along with his life savings, at a point on or near the creek beneath two large walnut trees.

Since that time, no one is sure exactly when the sightings began although the consensus of opinion is about the 1880s or 1890s — up until the 1930s — Nell frequently "reappeared,"

1

mostly through the psychic manifestation of knockings or rappings, to area oystermen. She was, apparently, a friendly ghost, who provided timely news on where the best oystering was from day to day, and she often played games in which she seemed to enjoy answering questions, mostly concerning numbers and figures. Why she chose to befriend the lonely watermen is a question that remains unanswered.

But from here, the tale is best told by a very real, 79-year-old former oysterman and life-long resident of Poquoson who we shall call "J.P." He doesn't want his real name used because he is afraid the relating of his experience will subject him to crank calls. J.P. is, of course, retired now, but for many years in the 1920s and 1930s, he worked the waters of the James with his father and his brother.

"I definitely believe she was there. There's no doubt in my mind," he says of Nell. "I'm not a superstitious person, or necessarily a believer in ghosts, but in this instance I do believe. I only experienced her presence once, but it was something I will never forget. My father and brother heard her many times, and they believed. And I know they wouldn't tell a lie for anyone. Many say it was a myth, but a lot of people heard her."

As J.P. tells it, the stories about Nell began occurring late in the 19th century. No one ever saw her. They heard her. She "appeared" by knocking on the cabin roofs of the oystermen's boats.

"It was a knock unlike any other I have ever heard," J.P. recalls. It was different. I can't even describe it. I guess I was about 18 or 20 when I experienced it. We were laid up overnight in the cove and I was standing outside the cabin with my head tucked inside, listening to the conversation. The cabin was full of watermen, talking. There was a very distinct knocking on top of the cabin. When I poked my head outside, it sounded like it came from outside. And when I ducked my head inside the cabin, it sounded like it came from the inside. There was no way it could have been a hoax. I wasn't really scared, but I must have looked concerned, because someone laughed and said, 'that's just ole Nell'."

J.P. says his father told him many times about the rappings. "He would never volunteer to talk about her, but if someone asked, he would tell you." What J.P.'s father said was that Nell

2

communicated only about things in the past. She would never "discuss" anything in the future.

She talked through her knockings. One rap meant yes, and two was for no. "In those days, people oystered over many sites up and down the James," J.P. continues. "Some would come out of the Warwick River, Deep Creek, Squashers Hole and other places. Every rock in the river had a name and the oystermen knew them all. So they would ask Nell how their peers were doing at other locations. Like, they would ask her, how many bushels of oysters did they get today at Thomas' rock (near the James River Bridge). And Nell would give so many knocks."

If the harvests were better elsewhere, according to J.P., then those asking the questions of Nell would fish those waters the next day. Invariably, their hauls improved. "Only a few of the men took stock in this," J.P. says, "but those who did always benefited from the advice. And she was always right. If she said so many bushels were brought in at such and such a rock, it was so."

Nell apparently amazed the men with all sorts of revelations. "She could answer anything she was asked," J.P. says. "You could ask her how many children someone had, and she would rap out the number in knocks on the cabin. You could ask her someone's age and she knew it exactly. My father said one time a man grabbed a handful of beans out of a sack and asked her how many he had. She told him, to the bean!"

In this manner, Nell carried on conversations with a number of oystermen over the years. She was especially conversant with one man, J.P. says, "and I was told that when he died she even appeared at his funeral by rapping on the coffin."

Robert Forrest, another life-long resident of Poquoson, well remembers his ancestors talking about Nell. "Oh, yes," he says, "I've heard the stories. The one I remember best concerned an old man named John, who was a very religious fellow. He had heard about Nell, too, and he didn't believe the stories until the night he experienced the sensation himself. He went out with some oystermen one time just to prove there was nothing to the tale. He carried his Bible with him.

"Well," Forrest continues, "they laid up in the Deep Creek area that night and tried to rouse her. 'Nell,' they said, 'if you're here, rap twice on the cabin.' Nothing happened. About 30

3

minutes later they tried again, and, sure enough, this time there were two sharp raps. They asked her several questions and she responded to each of them, but John still wasn't convinced. He thought someone was playing a trick on them, so he went out on deck. There was no one there and no boats nearby. Not only that, but the boat John was on had been untied from its stakes and was drifting freely in the creek. John became a believer right there!"

Occasionally, Nell would become disturbed at something asked or said, and she would quickly make her displeasure known. Randolph Rollins, a retired Poquoson carpenter, said he heard oystermen tell of the time she rocked their boat so violently they thought the tong shafts in the cabin would break. Yet, outside, the waters of the creek were "as smooth as a dish."

J.P. says his brother was reading the Bible to her one night, the chapter of Deuteronomy, when the knockings on the cabin became louder and louder and "got out of control." He stopped reading, and she stopped. "He never read the Bible to her again," J.P. says. Deuteronomy, it may be remembered, includes the ten commandments among which are "Thou shalt not kill," and "Honor thy father (and mother)." No wonder Nell was disturbed.

"All she ever told us was that her father had killed her and buried her nearby with his money," J.P. adds. "So one time, my father and brother went off digging in an area where there were two large walnut trees. Except the whole time they were there, they were pestered by large hornets or wasps, and they had to give it up."

Rollins tells of others who went looking for the lost loot. "One time they were driven off by a swarm of bees. They took that as an omen. Another time, a sudden storm whipped up and the wind nearly took down one of the trees. That scared them off and they never came back."

J.P., however, is not discouraged by all that. He is one who thinks there really is money buried somewhere in the Nell's Creek vicinity. "If I could, I would spend every penny I had to buy some land there now," he says. "But, of course, you can't. The government owns it. I tell you, though, I would like to pitch a tent right under those trees and spend the night. I sure wish I could talk to ole Nell again. I've tried many times, but she's never answered."

In fact, no one has heard from Nell for a number of years. She was a friend of the oystermen for a half century or so, but when the military took over at Ft. Eustis, the knockings ceased. "She must be at peace now," J.P. surmises.

CHAPTER 2

What bade me pause

before that garden-gate,

To breathe the incense of

those slumbering roses?

(*To Helen*)

The Psychic Wonders of White Marsh

ou have probably seen White Marsh in the movies — and not realized it! This magnificent, white-porticoed mansion, described as the "epitome of Southern plantations," and known as the "Queen of Tidewater," has, in fact, been the setting for a number of major films over the years. Contrary to some local belief, Gone With The Wind scenes were not shot here, but considerable footage for a number of other movies and TV dramas has been.

And no wonder. At first sight, even today, one might well expect a Southern belle in hoop-skirted gown, escorted by a tall gentleman resplendent in an ivory-colored suit and wide-brimmed hat, to appear on the front steps. White Marsh has that effect on first-time visitors.

Situated strategically back from the Ware River in Gloucester, White Marsh stands amid a grant of land originally made in the 1640s. There are conflicting reports about exactly when the Georgian Colonial mansion was built by Major Lewis Burwell; some say about 1735, others about 1750. In time, the estate passed to Evelina Mathilda Prosser, who married John Tabb, son of Phillip Tabb of Toddsbury. After adding his wife's fortune to his own, John Tabb was said to have been the wealthiest man in Gloucester. Evelina has been described as a woman of great dignity, often gowned in black moire antique.

There were then 3,000 acres in the White Marsh Plantation, worked by from 300 to 500 slaves. In fact, 1,500 slaves rest in a graveyard near the peach orchard. This vast expanse included forest land, farm land, lawns, gardens and orchards, and in the rich marl, excellent crops of corn and soybeans were harvested. The house itself was framed by giant boxwoods and flanked by what is said to have been the largest ginkgo tree in the country.

Despite all this splendor, however, Mrs. Tabb, it was said, was not happy with the bucolic life. She had lost two of her children in infancy, and wanted to move to Norfolk or Williamsburg to enjoy a gayer social life. Mr. Tabb did not want to move, and he told his wife if she would make herself content and remain in the country, he would create the finest garden in Virginia for her. It was then that the terraced gardens were built, and many rare and fine trees were planted in the park. The house also was remodeled, and wings and a pillared portico were added.

While Evelina, also affectionately known as "Mother Tabb," was pleased with her garden, there are indications she was never totally happy at White Marsh. The deaths of her two infant children sent her into long periods of mourning. It was shortly after she and John passed on that the "occurrences" began. Phillip Tabb inherited the plantation from his parents, and as he lived in Baltimore, he placed it under the care of James Sinclair, returning only occasionally, with guests, during the fox hunting season.

Late one evening, Sinclair, returning to the house from town on horseback, was astonished to find every window ablaze with light. Fearing his boss had come back without notice, he stabled his horse and rushed up the steps. The house was now dark and no one was inside. Curiously, the next year, the same thing happened to a caretaker named Franklin Dabney. He, too, approached White Marsh after being away one night, and not only found every window lighted, but he clearly heard music and the sound of dancing. A bachelor, he bounded up the porch steps to participate in the merry-making. But when he opened the door, there was only darkness and silence!

Years later, the Rev. William Byrd Lee, then rector emeritus of Ware Church, and his wife paid a call to White Marsh and were greeted by Catherine Tabb, granddaughter of Evelina.

As they prepared to leave, the Reverend went to bring his buggy to the door, and Mrs. Lee was seated alone in the hall. She happened to glance up the staircase, and her heart froze. She saw an elderly lady of "stately and distinguished appearance and carriage" descending the stairs. She was dressed in an old fashioned costume of black moire antique! She had a white fichu around her shoulders, and she carried a leather key basket, common for the mistress of a plantation. The figure crossed the hall and disappeared into the dining room. It was then that Mrs. Lee suddenly realized the figure was "not that of a mortal".

She called to her hostess and excitedly told her what she had just witnessed. To her surprise, Catherine Tabb just laughed and then explained that it was just Mother Tabb, who was often seen by members of the family. It was some time before Mrs. Lee made a return visit to White Marsh.

A generation later, in 1984, Eliza A. Lee, then 92, and the daughter of Mrs. Lee, confirmed the story. She is convinced her mother believed she saw Evelina. "She never knew the woman had been seen by others; she wouldn't have framed her remarks to the lady of the house the way she did if she had been aware of a ghostly presence," Miss Lee told a newspaper reporter. "She didn't say she'd 'seen the ghost', which would have indicated she'd heard the story before.

Members of the Tabb household also reported seeing Evelina

enter a certain bedroom, open the lowest drawer of a bureau and remove all the infant clothes inside it. Ever so carefully, she would take each article, shake it, refold it and place it back in the bureau. She then would quietly slip out of the room.

And then there was the resistant rose bush. This occurred some years later, after the home had passed from the Tabbs to a "Mr. & Mrs. Hughes" from New York. The pride of the garden was the proliferation of magnificent rose bushes. One May they were full of buds and on the second terrace was an especially luxuriant bush on which Mrs. Hughes found a full-blown rose with rich, creamy petals.

As she reached out to pick it, a most extraordinary thing happened. The bush began swaying violently as if whipped by a strong wind. Mrs. Hughes looked around in dismay. There was not a breeze stirring. She tried again and again the bush trembled as if being shaken by unseen hands. Perturbed, she grabbed the stem firmly, but the rose was snatched from her hand and it began swaying again. At this, the shutters of the house commenced banging sharply.

She fled to the house in terror and told her husband about it. He confidently approached the bush, but the same thing happened again. A prudent man, he left it alone, fearing if he did pick the rose something disagreeable might happen. In time, the incident spread through the county and many visitors came to see the reluctant bush.

Servants contended it was the hand of Mother Tabb which had intervened. They said that had been her favorite rose and she allowed no one to snip it. Mrs. Hughes eventually grew nervous over the phenomenon, coupled with the banging shutters, and she ordered that the bush be destroyed. Soon after, as she was making her rounds of the garden one morning, she found the rosebush gone, roots and all.

She asked the gardener if he had dug it up as she had commanded. He told her, "No"!

And finally there is this ancestrally-related postscript, which took place some years after Evelina's death. It was at Belle Ville, another picturesque mansion dating to 1658 on the North River in Gloucester County. there, the master of the house, Warner Taliaferro, of Church Hill, had fallen asleep on the porch while worrying about the grave illness of a neighbor, Mrs. Tabb, the wife of one of Evelina's descendants.

Late in the night, he was awakened by "a light touch." Startled, he sat up and saw what appeared to be Mrs. Tabb on the steps leading down into his garden. Afraid she had somehow gotten out of her sick bed and was wandering about in delirium, he got up and followed the nebulous figure. She glided down a walk, crossed over a lawn, knelt down by a crepe myrtle, and then went into the summer house. Taliaferro entered the building seconds later only to find it empty.

He raced back to Belle Ville, woke his wife, and recounted the ethereal-like experience. She told him he must have been dreaming. He said for her to feel his clothes. They were drenched with the dew from the tall grass.

The next morning a messenger brought news of Mrs. Tabb's death. It coincided exactly with the time Taliaferro had seen the apparition!

* * * * *

In 1948, Constance Ingles moved into the house. Although she is modest about it, she is sensitive to psychic phenomena, and had once seen a ghost when she was a 16-year-old student at Bennington College West, in New York State. About three or four weeks after moving in with her family, she was awakened one night by "heavy footsteps" tramping about in the attic. She was reluctant to wake her husband, a disbeliever, but then her four-year-old daughter called out to her asking who was up in the attic.

Constance then woke her husband, and he heard the sounds, too. As they got out of bed to investigate, something seemed to land on the roof of the one-story wing right under their bedroom window. As they looked out the window they heard a loud "thud" smack the ground below. Seconds later, they heard the distinct sound of horses' hoofs heading up the lane. They found nothing amiss in the house, but the next morning they saw hoof-prints outside, directly under their window. They looked in the barn, but all their horses were there.

About a year later, the Ingles hired a black couple from Philadelphia named Henry and Frances Parker. They were, Constance says, unaware of the ghostly legends at White Marsh. Soon after their arrival, Henry came to Constance one Sunday morning and asked if she and her husband, who had been away, had come home unexpectedly the previous afternoon. She told him that they hadn't and asked him why he wanted to know.

He said it was because on that Saturday afternoon, while the house was empty, he and his wife had heard someone playing the piano. Henry had thought the Ingles had come home early, but his wife said it didn't sound like Mrs. Ingles' playing. He then decided to check it out and when he reached the stair landing, near the piano, the music stopped mysteriously, and there was what he described as a "whooshing sound" that moved past him toward a door to the back hall.

A week later, Henry appeared shaken as he served Constance morning coffee. He said that he and his wife had not slept at all the previous night because something was "rocking" in their room. This, Constance declared, was quite strange, because there was no rocking chair in the room. Henry acknowledged this, but told her that a straight chair seemed "to rock as if it had rockers under it." Constance told these stories to Hans Holzer, the famous ghost expert, who wrote about them in his book "The Phantoms of Dixie," published in 1972.

Constance today says that things have been quiet, psychically at least, at White Marsh over the past few years. "Oh, there are a few weird things that happen every now and then, but not much out of the ordinary," she says. It seems that the spirit, or spirits, seem content to co-exist peacefully.

The Resplendent Ruins of Rosewell

Rosewell!

Today, more than two and a half centuries after its construction began just off the northern shores of the York River in Gloucester County, the name Rosewell still evokes excitement, even though it has stood in ruins since being gutted in a 1916 fire.

The accolades of its once-magnificent presence continue to ring true. Says Claude Lanciano, Jr., author of "Rosewell, Garland of Virginia:" "The masterpiece called Rosewell at the height of its glory, in mid-eighteenth century, knew few rivals and has been called by many the finest example of colonial architecture in America."

Adds Williamsburg author-historian Parke Rouse: "Rosewell had a glorious heyday. The Palladian mansion was a showplace, frequented by Tidewater nabobs." Thomas Tileston Waterman, the eminent architectural historian, said, "It was the largest and finest of American houses of the Colonial period." Rosewell also has been called "a crossroads of American history for nearly three centuries." Possibly the finest tribute was paid by noted American artist James Reynolds, who once said: "I regard Rosewell as the finest house in Palladian style I have ever seen in this country. I would rather own it, ruinous as it stands, than any other in the United States."

Construction on this palatial brick masterpiece began in 1725 under its land owner, Mann Page. Built in the style of a Georgian town house which slightly resembled the Governor's Palace in Williamsburg, it stood four stories high with white marble casements and two turrets on the roof, inside of which were little rooms. These turrets had windows on all four sides which made excellent lookouts. A pitched roof supported massive chimneys. From the lantern windows, one was treated to a superb panorama of meadowland, low hills, and the misty reaches of the York River and of Carter's Creek. Two one-story quadrant connections joined the pavilions that projected from the east and west facade to a pair of dependencies. Each of these amounted to a good-sized house of one and a half stories, embracing five dormer windows across the roof.

The interior plan of Rosewell showed five large rooms on the first floor. On the second was a huge apartment used as a ballroom. In all, the house consisted of 35 rooms, three wide halls and nine passageways. It was full of beautifully carved staircases, mantels, and paneling that is said to have been exquisite beyond description. The entrance hall had full-height pilasters, and the immensely high stairwell extended from the first floor to the rooftop. It could be ascended by eight people abreast. The balustrade of the stairs was elegantly carved with designs of baskets of fruit and flowers.

Mann Page never lived to see his great house finished. His son, Mann Page II, completed it in 1744. A generation later Thomas Jefferson spent a great deal of time at Rosewell as the guest of his friend John Page. There are some who say Jefferson even penned a draft of the Declaration of Independence at Rosewell, but this is unsubstantiated.

In its time, Rosewell was known throughout Virginia and the east coast for the lavish parties and balls that were thrown there, attended by aristocratic gentlemen and hoop-skirted, velvet dressed Southern Belles. Casks of the finest French wines, and magnums of champagne were brought in by boat to wash down gourmet meals fit for a king. Scores of garlands of flowers, especially roses, richly decorated every room, and dances lasted till nearly dawn. It was a grand time.

But Rosewell had a dark side, too. Parke Rouse said the plantation was "ill-starred". In retrospect, it could be compared in a way with the fictional Tara of Margaret Mitchell's "Gone With The Wind". There is even a Scarlett O'Hara type character associated with Rosewell, and therein lies a haunting tale well worth the retelling.

It occurred sometime during the period of occupancy by Mann Page II, probably about the middle of the 18th century. Anne Page, the renowned hostess at Rosewell, announced a ball. It was the talk of Gloucester for weeks in advance. Amid the society gossip was the speculation as to whether or not Letitia Dalton would attend. Letitia was the "Scarlett" of that day who lived with her husband, Fairfax, at nearby Paynton

13

Plantation. Two days prior to the ball, her sister, Caro, had died under the most mysterious circumstances.

Letitia had commanded her to go outside the house to fetch her some grapes in the midst of a ferocious storm. Caro never returned to the house that night. They found her body the next morning. Some said a tree limb crushed her skull. Others contended she had stumbled into a pile of cut glass, severed arteries, and bled to death. Whatever, it was widely known that Letitia and Caro hated each other, and often had raging arguments. There was talk that Letitia had somehow engineered her sister's death.

And so it came with some surprise, and considerable indignation among the guests, that Letitia not only showed up for the ball, but as Scarlett did on so many occasions, she stole the show. Just before dinner, long after everyone had gathered downstairs, she made her flamboyant entrance, descending the staircase in a wide-hooped gown of rose-pink satin with panniers of rose-latticed lace. Her powdered hair was massed with roses and plumes of rose color in the Versailles style.

Not only had she captivated the men at the ball, at the expense and disdain of their ladies, which mattered not the least to Letitia, but she spent a good part of the evening ignoring her husband and flirting with a handsome Englishman, Captain Godfrey Chandos, heir to a dukedom. Her behavior was, in a word, scandalous. She rejoiced in it.

Nor was it any secret that she made Fairfax's life miserable, often driving him from the house in total frustration with her merciless, deceitful harangues. He, in fact, spent much of his time in consolation with his good friends, the Pages, at Rosewell.

No sooner had the talk of Caro's untimely death died down when tragedy struck again at Paynton. Fairfax Dalton had retired to his bedroom one evening when it was reported that he heard a soft voice calling from the bottom of the stair well. "Fairfax. Here. Fairfax, I am here," he heard faintly. Sensing a note of fear and urgency, he went to the top of the staircase and peered downward into the lurking darkness. "Here I am. Look over here," he heard. As he leaned hard on the balustrade, the wooden railing collapsed and he plummeted head first down two stories onto the marble floor. He died of a broken neck.

14

There were no witnesses. Letitia claimed to have been asleep in her own room, but opinion was rampant that she had been the one who called Fairfax to his death.

She was also believed to have directly caused two other deaths at Paynton. She once sent a servant named Tacton out into driving spring rains to retrieve a runaway mare. He returned to tell her he had sighted the mare, marooned on a small sandbar surrounded by quicksand bogs. Despite the obvious dangers, she ordered him to bring the mare home. Neither he nor the horse were ever seen again.

In the other instance, Letitia, greedy for strong slaves to work her fields, ordered Clairy, a housemaid, to send her child Clarisse to the cabin of a strong black stud slave, even through the girl, probably 10 or 11 at the time, was too young to conceive. In the brutal raping that followed, Clarisse died from loss of blood.

With these two deaths combined with those of Caro and Fairfax, Letitia was labeled a murderess, but ironically, she was never called to answer any charges. She died of natural causes in her bed. Her gruesome legacy, however, lived on. For years afterward, guests at Paynton Hall told of seeing a small, shadowy figure of a woman passing through darkened halls. As she went by, they felt a sudden push or a tripping of their feet. One lady saved herself from hurtling down the stairs by grasping a newel post.

Others heard horrible cries ring through the house late at night, and there were oft-told stories of blood on the marble floor impossible to rub clean. In 1840, it was reported, slaves refused to stay in the huts near the old stud cabin, saying they had seen a Negro woman, crouched on the floor of the cabin wailing over a young girl who was covered with blood. The superintendent told of hearing sobs of terrible anguish coming from the cabin late at night.

And, years after her tragic death, a story surfaced explaining what happened to Caro. It was widely surmised that Letitia had, in fact, gone out earlier in the night, as a fierce storm was brewing, and had piled shards of glass above a spot where the finest grapes hung in clusters. The roof was shored by rickety planks, and she had wrenched them loose. Then, she placed a loose board in such a position that anyone stumbling over it would send the shoring, glass and all, showering down on them. Then, later in the evening, when the wind was howling at its worst, she had sent Caro upon her fatal mission.

At last, Paynton Hall was burned to the ground during the Civil War battle of York Plains Ford. Nothing but grass-grown foundations remain. The voices, cries of anguish and

apparitions, too, have disappeared.

But others have resurfaced at nearby Rosewell. Many Gloucester natives have told stories of strange sightings and noises emanating from the rose-red brick foundation ruins. Some claim to have seen young boy servants standing beside the great pedimented doorway at night, lighting the way for arriving distinguished guests who vanish ascending the Corinthian pilastered stair well. Others swear they hear violin and harpsichord music rising above the towering chimneys.

Ronnie Miles, an office worker in Williamsburg and a native of Mathews County, had two psychic experiences at Rosewell about 20 years ago. Once, he and a friend were exploring the ruins at night when they stumbled onto what may have been an entrance to a wine cellar. Miles' friend lit a match to see better, only to have a flung brick knock the match out of his hand. He never went back to Rosewell, even in daylight. "I have to admit, it scared the hell out of us," Miles said. "We had always heard a slave had been buried in the walls."

On the second occasion, Miles and another friend and two girls were walking through the old Rosewell cemetery at night, as teenagers sometimes do for kicks. Miles and his friend saw what appeared to be a light coming from the house ruins. Not wanting to scare the girls, they walked back to the site alone to investigate. "As we reached the perimeter of the ruins," said Miles, "we both were overcome by the most all-powerful stench I have ever smelled. It was potent. I have never smelled anything like it in my life. It literally drove us away."

Another chilling instance was experienced by John Gulbranson, an amateur psychic investigator, his sister, and some friends. As a hobby, Gulbranson and his brother, Tom, check out ghost stories, complete with sophisticated camera and tape recorder equipment. While in the Gloucester area one night several years ago, they decided to go look at the Rosewell ruins.

They drove down to the edge of two cornfields near the entrance road and got out there because the road had been chained to discourage visitors. They had two guard dogs with them, but the dogs immediately began howling wildly and refused to budge. "We tried to pull them, but we couldn't move them an inch," John says. Previously, the dogs had never exhibited fear.

The dogs were tied to a tree and the group walked through the cornfields and down the entrance road. A couple of the young men swore they heard the sounds of a drummer coming from the Rosewell site, but when they got there, they found nothing. They then retraced their steps back to the car and everyone got in. Just as they did the dogs began barking furiously at the back window and the hair on their backs stiffened.

John and the others looked out the window, and a few yards away they all clearly saw a black man suspended four or five feet above the ground. John's sister, Carol, began screaming hysterically, and they drove off, spinning their tires in the dirt.

They had the distinct feeling, the man, or whatever it was, was following them, so they sped so fast on the rough surface, their heads bumped against the roof of the car.

A mile or so down the road they stopped, got out and looked back. The man was gone. There was one small tree, only about an inch in diameter at the side of the road, which leaned out over the lane. Without warning, the tree began shaking violently, but they could see no cause for it.

Again, they jumped into the car and raced away. This time they didn't stop until they got back to civilization, and they pulled up under a street light. They got out and walked around the car. It was covered with dew. One of the group called the others to the rear of the car. There, in the dew, were the crystal-clear impressions of a baby's hand and a man's hand with a missing index finger!

But perhaps the most frightening phenomenon of all at Rosewell was experienced by Raymond West, a maintenance worker at a fiber plant in James City County. He and a friend were out joyriding with two young ladies when they decided to go visit the Rosewell ruins. It was about two in the morning and the story is best told in West's own words. "There was an old dirt road that ran for about half a mile leading up to the place," he recalls. "As we made the last turn to the left, there before us was an old black car with 1930s license plates blocking the driveway. It had old half moon windows in the back and was facing away from us. It stunned us. I slammed on the brakes, and a big dust cloud rose up then cleared, so you could see the car real well in the headlight beams. It was eerie.

"Then, as we sat there in silence, we saw the head of a woman rise up in the rear window and she stared at us. She had coal black hair and an ashen-white face. We panicked. I tried to get the car in reverse, but the gears kept sticking, and all the time that woman kept looking at us, unblinking. Finally, I got the car in gear and we burned rubber getting out of there. We pulled back a few hundred yards and then stopped. We were plenty scared, but we decided to wait until daylight and check things out. There was no other way out of there, no other roads, paths or anything. If that car left, it had to go right past us.

"At daybreak, we drove back down the driveway to the spot where we had seen it, and there was nothing there! The car and the woman had disappeared. There were no tracks or anything. We looked everywhere but could find nothing. I tell you, I never believed in ghosts or anything like that, but to this day I can't explain what we saw or why."

Could they have seen a manifestation of Letitia Dalton, returning to seek the attentions of the handsome British Captain who escaped her flirtations in life? Could that also explain one of the most common psychic sightings over the years at Rosewell — that of the figure of a woman in a red cloak running toward the grove where the roses once bloomed?

Could that possibly explain why the artist James Reynolds once wrote: "Certainly tremendous doings took place within the fire-riven walls of Rosewell . . . And what stories one hears of hauntings! All I hear seems in keeping with the magnificence and stature of this barren, deserted house."

CHAPTER 4

They weep: — from off
their delicate stems
Perennial tears descend
in gems

(The Valley of Unrest)

Tragic Teardrops in the Snow

If sad stories disturb you, perhaps it would be best to skip the following chapter, because this melancholy saga is definitely a two-or-three hanky affair. It begins with a broken heart, includes such grisly details as a premature burial, grave robbing, and a severed finger, and ends with tragic plea for help that was drowned out in a blinding snowstorm. In the world of the macabre it exceeds even the feverish imagination of Edgar Allen Poe. There is also an intriguing epilogue involving the lush seasonal growth of violets "watered by the tears of a dying girl."

If however, the above has piqued your interest, and you have the heart, read on.

The setting is Church Hill in Gloucester, where a large frame house stands today on an elevation just above the Ware River. In 1650, a grant of 1,174 acres was given to Mordecai Cooke, who later became a member of the House of Burgesses, and who once served as sheriff of Gloucester. In 1658 a brick house was built at this site and was known as "Mordecai's Mount". In the 1700s, the main part of the house burned, leaving a brick wing. Later, this, too, burned and an entirely new frame house was constructed on the old foundations and became known as Church Hill.

The Cooke property passed in a direct line to descendants named Throckmorton. Then one of the two heiresses of the house married William Taliaferro, and when she died, her sister married the widower. Both the Throckmortons and the Taliaferros produced a number of distinguished citizens in Colonial days.

One of the Throckmortons had a beautiful daughter named Elizabeth, which is somewhat strange in itself, because one writer reported there is no record of an Elizabeth Throckmorton at Church Hill. Whatever her name was, her father took her for a visit to London where she met a handsome young English gentleman, with whom she fell deeply in love. They both declared eternal faithfulness to each other and arranged to complete plans for their wedding by correspondence. Elizabeth's father, however, was staunchly against the match, and intercepted the letters, so neither ever heard again from the other after Elizabeth had returned to Gloucester.

In time, as Elizabeth longed for her lost love, she fell ill and, apparently, died. Friends contended she had lost the will to live, and "pined away". On a blustery November afternoon near sunset, they buried her in the graveyard at the foot of the garden.

According to one account, an evil butler, angered at some slight accorded him by the family, dug up her gravesite that night and opened the coffin to steal valuable jewelry that had been buried with Elizabeth. One particular ring would not slip

off her stiffened finger, and in his haste, the servant severed the finger.

To his horror, however, he found the girl was not dead! She had lapsed into a cataleptic coma and had been presumed dead. The shock of having her finger cut off roused her, and the terrified butler ran off into the night never to be heard from again.

Somehow, the frail girl, barefoot and thinly dressed, managed to climb out of the grave, crawl past the last dead stalks of the garden, and drag herself through a driving snowstorm — the first snow of the season — to the house. There, in a weakened condition, she scratched feebly at the door. If her father, sitting inside before a roaring fire, heard her, he dismissed it as one of the dogs trying to come in out of the storm, and, lost in his grief, ignored the sound.

The next morning, Elizabeth's body was found at the doorstep beneath a blanket of snow. She had frozen to death. There was a trail of bloody footprints leading from the garden.

For years afterward, succeeding generations of Throckmortons and Taliaferros swore that manifestations of Elizabeth were present in the house. Whenever the first snow fell, each year, there would be sounds of a rustling skirt ascending the staircase, followed by the distinct placing of logs in fireplaces and the crackle of a hearty fire in various rooms. Investigations would find no such logs and no fires. There also would be traces of blood in the snow following the route Elizabeth had taken from the graveyard to the house. Such sounds and sights were experienced not once, but many times, and were attested to by various members of the family and their servants.

On one noteworthy occasion, generations later, in 1879, Professor Warner Taliaferro, then head of the house, left home one evening to spend the night at a friend's home. Neighbors reported, that in the midst of a fierce storm, they saw Church Hill ablaze with lights. Junius Browne Jr., passing by on horseback, rode up to the house to see if his sisters, visiting in the neighborhood, had sought shelter from the storm there. There was no one home. Servants living in their quarters on the property, also saw the lights and had assumed Mr. Taliaferro had returned. He had not. This mystery was never explained.

But the most telling phenomenon concerns the violets, which grow in lush profusion near the steps to Church Hill.

They are finer and more beautiful here than those in any other parts of the grounds. It is said they were watered by the tears of a dying girl seeking refuge from the season's first snow!

A Galaxy of Gloucester Ghosts

Why are there so many reports of ghosts in the Gloucester area? Literally, dozens of houses have stories to tell. Of course, the county contains many old mansions predating the Revolutionary War, and the history of the area runs rich from Colonial days long past the Civil War, providing fertile grounds for such tales.

At Level Green, built in 1692, for example, the apparition of Anna Fahs, who died very young, is said to roam about. At Sherwood, the spectral image of a wounded Federal officer, befriended by the owners during the War between the States, appears on the front porch to ward off malicious intruders. And stately old Airville, whose ownership once was lost in a poker game in the mid-1800s, reputedly has a "benevolent ghost."

Then there are the better known and somewhat better documented cases of strange happenings at White Marsh, Rosewell, and Church Hill. Herewith, is a sampling of other spiritual sights, sounds and scenes of Gloucester.

* * * * *

The Apparition at Abingdon Church

It is worth the trip just to see the splendid old church and to casually stroll through the adjacent cemetery which contains a number of tombstones with coats of arms carved upon them. Abingdon Church is said to have been planned by Sir Christopher Wren, the famous architect. It was built in 1755, in the form of a Greek cross, and replaced an earlier church that had stood since the mid-17th century. Abingdon is notable for an elaborate reredos representing in bas-relief the facade of a Greek temple.

For generations, many rich and aristocratic families worshipped here. Peculiarly, the building had no heat, and in the winter servants placed hot bricks at the pew owners' feet for warmth, while the less-endowed members of the congregation shivered. The silver service, still in use, was presented by Major Lewis Burwell of Carter's Creek in 1703. Some of the old box pews were used by the British as box stalls for horses during the Revolutionary War.

But the single ghostly tale about Abingdon, eloquently described by Caroline Baytop Sinclair in her interesting book "Stories of Old Gloucester," pertains to the Civil War. It occurred, as Ms. Sinclair wrote, on "a stormy, wet night in 1863." A lone, young Federal calvaryman was returning to his station at Gloucester Point late that night, tired, cold, wet and "disgruntled." He had become separated from his party and he and his horse had stumbled through grapevines, poison ivy and briar patches in their efforts to evade the Confederate enemy.

Near midnight, the storm intensified, and the soldier sought shelter. He came upon Abingdon Church and led his horse through the large doors and onto the stone floors. The building had recently been occupied by troops, and by the flashes of

lightning, he could see it was in "desolate disorder"; pews and paneling were broken and charred wood and ashes were scattered on the floor.

But he sensed something else, too. In the intermittent light of the storm he perceived something moving in the north gallery. As his eyes adjusted, it appeared to be tall, white and descending the stairway. When another bolt pierced the sky revealing the filmy apparition of a human-like form, the soldier had seen enough. He mounted up and his horse clattered through the arched door and across the churchyard. Too late! As Sinclair told it, "the flashing streaks in the sky revealed two riders upon the horse's back."

* * * * *

Lost Love at Auburn

And so, all the night-tide, I lie

down by the side of my darling

— my darling — my life and

my bride

(Annibel Lee)

ven if there hadn't been a ghost associated with Auburn, a magnificent home on the North River in Mathews County, there should have been. Fortunately for this story, there was and is. This Georgian-style showpiece was built in 1804 by Phillip Tabb of Toddsbury for his son, Dr. Henry Wythe Tabb, who was married three times and had seven daughters and two sons.

The mansion features brick walls three feet thick and mantels, stairs and panels of exquisite hand-carved mahogany. It also reputedly had the first flush toilet in Mathews, which could be found halfway up the staircase to the third floor. The roof of the house has a walk around it, like houses in New England, made of cypress transported from the Dismal Swamp. The lawn, from which there is an excellent river view, is dominated by a towering great oak tree and noble elms.

One of the latter day owners of Auburn was Beatle John Lennon, who was gunned down outside his New York City residence, the Dakota House, in 1980. Dakota, too, is said to be haunted with many spirits. In fact, Lennon's assassin, Mark David Chapman, told police he "heard voices" just before the shooting.

The key reason Auburn should be haunted, is the ironic tragedy that occurred there in the middle of the 19th century. Even Shakespeare himself would have had trouble imagining such a scenario. It involved one of Henry Tabb's daughters, Eliza. As she ascended the stairs on her wedding day, she tripped on her gown, fell and died, likely of a broken neck. This documented fact made up the central plot of author Joseph Hergesheimer's novel, "Balisand".

Ever since that time, Eliza's beaded slippers, part of her wedding ensemble, have been passed down from owner to owner at Auburn in a peculiar tradition.

Many people have reported strange sounds in the house which they have connected with the unfortunate bride, but Peggy Licht thinks otherwise. She believes they are made by the fiancee who comes back in search of his lost Eliza. Peggy and her husband, Tom, were caretakers at Auburn for four years, right after Oko Lennon sold the place.

"I've heard steps," she says, "and they do seem to be much heavier than those a petite young bride might make. While we were there, we had a number of guests, none of whom knew anything about the legend, report hearing the steps on the winding stairwell and doors slamming in the night. Most of them got out of bed to see who it was. Nobody saw anything.

"The other site where the groom's presence often has been felt is under the great oak tree," Peggy adds. "This is where Eliza and her beau met to make their wedding plans. You can feel frigid spots of air, even on the hottest days of summer under that tree. And it wasn't just me. Others have experienced it, too. An Episcopal minister visited once, and he told me about suddenly feeling chilled. It's eerie."

* * * * *

A Reunion in the Beyond

Another tragic love story is told about Midlothian, a graceful house on the

North River in Gloucester County built in 1752 by Josiah Lilly Deans. A family named Iverson owned this 1,200-acre spread for some time and there is word that young Hubert Iverson had a sweetheart named Jennie Bower, a country girl, but their love could not be consummated, at least not in earthly terms.

Dying of fever, Hubert begged his parents to take care of Jennie, but they refused his deathbed request, and not long after he departed this earth, she passed away, supposedly of grief and privation.

Almost immediately thereafter, the survivors at Midlothian, including the servants, saw apparitions of the spirit couple, walking hand in hand down corridors and through the garden. And at night, family members were often awakened by sounds of moaning and groaning described as "pitiful and distressing."

Taunted by guilty consciences, the Iversons sold the house to the Marables, and they also experienced the ghostly visitations. Deeply religious and disturbed, they called in the rector of Petsworth Parish, the Reverend Robert Yates, to undertake an exorcism. At that time, such practice consisted of consigning troubled spirits to burial under water.

On the appointed day, Rev. Yates assembled the family, neighbors and servants. Together, they walked backwards toward a well in an adjacent field, as the burial service according to the rites of the Anglican Church was repeated. Prayers and the solemn vows of exorcism were spoken as the group stood around the well, in a traditional ceremony complete with bell, book and candle. Then the well was filled in.

The lovers were never seen or heard from again!

* * * * *

The Ethereal Visitor at Enfield

here is a legend about Enfield, another fine old Gloucester home, that dates to pre-Civil War days. While the details are sketchy, the story revolves around one-time Enfield master James Catlett and his favorite slave. One or the other, allegedly still roams the grounds. There certainly would be just cause, for what follows is a tragic tale.

Catlett owned a fine gold watch and made the mistake of telling his servant, who had often admired it, that he would leave it to him when he died. The slave couldn't wait. When they were both chopping wood in the field one day, the servant slipped up behind Catlett and split his skull with a sharp axe. He took the watch and then dismembered the body and buried the pieces, later telling people at the house that the master has been detained.

When Catlett didn't show up searchers scoured the fields, and, with the aid of a pointer dog, uncovered the grisly remains. The slave confessed and was tried and sentenced in the Gloucester County Court and hanged on the Court green. There is confusion as to exactly who the apparition sighted at Enfield really is: James Catlett, returning in disbelief, or the servant, doomed to roam the grounds in repentance.

* * * * *

Cries from
Another World

A more modern episode, and though inexplicable, possibly more believable, is recounted by Tom Gulbranson, an office supply salesman who has spent the past 20 years tracking down ghostly phenomena as a hobby. As Tom tells it, it involved tragedy and heartbreak in a house in Bellamy Manor, about two miles distant from the famous ruins of Rosewell. What he pieced together was that a jealous husband killed his wife's lover. Soon after, the couple's small child died, and not long after that, the disconsolate wife died. From that time on, sounds of a baby crying and a mother looking for it emanated from the house.

Tom and some of his friends went to investigate the now-empty house in the early 1970s. they set up their psychic sensing equipment, including a tape recorder. There were no sounds heard during their hours in the house. Disappointed, they packed up their gear and went home.

The next morning Tom was rudely awakened by his mother's screams. They had told her about their trip the previous night, and that morning she played the tape. On it was the distinct sound of a baby crying!

* * * * *

Arisen from a Watery Grave

ne definition of precognition is that it is clairvoyance relating to an event or state not yet experienced. That might explain what happened to Ed Jenkins' aunt one stormy night during the 1920s. Ed, a native of Guinea, east of Gloucester Point, is also quoted in the chapter in this book on "Strange Lights in the Night." He says his father and his aunt, Irving and Clarisse, were living near the Point at that time, and she was being courted by a young man who crossed the York River near Cheatham Annex by boat, as this was long before the era of the Coleman Bridge.

On this particular night he failed to show up. Late in the evening, Clarise went into the kitchen and screamed in terror. there, outside the window, was the pale, ghostly face of her suitor — at an elevation of about 10 feet off the ground. Irving searched the grounds and found nothing, not even footprints.

He went back into the house, got his shotgun, loaded it, and went outside again. Apparently, according to Ed, there was an old-time tradition that if you fired your shotgun into the air, it would ward off evil spirits. He pulled the trigger time after time, but it wouldn't go off. Ed says his father told him that each time the firing pin hit the cap of the shell, actually making an indentation in it, but it wouldn't fire.

The next morning Irving tried again, and shotgun roared without trouble. Then, later in the day, they got the word. Clarise's beau had drowned in the York during the previous night's storm.

And Thou, a ghost,

amid the entombing

trees Didst glide away

(To Helen)

The Multiple Mysteries of Old House Woods

f all the ghostly tales of Tidewater, perhaps none is more widely known, or has been told, retold, written and rewritten more often than Old House Woods, also called Old Haunted Woods, near the tiny crossroads town of Diggs in Mathews County, northeast of Gloucester.

And for good reason. The colorful stories that have been passed down from generation to generation for more than 200 years about this 50 acre patch of pine woods and marshlands near the Chesapeake Bay contain some of the most bizarre and unusual psychic phenomena ever recorded. They are, in fact, so strange that one tends to lend some credence to them, because even the most fertile imagination would have difficulty dreaming them up.

They include all the elements of the creative thrillers of Robert Louis Stevenson and Edgar Allan Poe combined! Consider for example: swashbuckling pirates burying stolen gold; retreating British soldiers hiding colonial treasure during the Revolutionary War; a full-rigged Spanish galleon which vanishes in thin air; skeletons in knights' armor wielding threatening swords; mysterious groups of shovelers digging furiously late at night; ghost horses and cows which appear and disappear before one's eyes.

"Yes, it's true. All those stories and more have come out of Old House Woods," says Olivia Davis, a lifelong resident.

She should know, as well as anyone still alive. Her great, great grandfather, James Forrest, bought this land in 1838 and it was kept in the family and farmed for more than 100 years. She still has the original, handwritten deed.

Old House Woods got its name, simply enough, from a large frame house, once known as the Fannie Knight house, which had a wood-covered plaster chimney, and stood in the midst of the forest in the late 1700s. Later, after being abandoned for years, it fell into disrepair, and thereafter became known as "the Old House."

"What you have to remember is that in the days before television and even radio, telling tales was a popular pastime, particularly in this area," Olivia says. "Old timers used to gather in the woods on Sundays and swap yarns. The best story teller was the one who could best hold your interest. I can well recall my grandfather, Silas Forrest talking about ghosts and it was spellbinding."

Does she believe they were true? "I consider them just exactly what they are — stories."

But there are scores of others, residents and visitors to the area alike, who swear by them. And then there are those who have personally experienced the phenomena in one form or another. There is no way they will ever be shaken from their beliefs. They were there. They saw for themselves. And they never forgot, carrying their terrified memories to the grave.

There are, allegedly, three reasons why Old House Woods are haunted. According to one legend, the crew of a pirate ship came ashore here in the 17th century, buried their treasure somewhere deep in the woods, then returned to sea where they perished in a furious storm. That explains, say proponents of this theory, why mysterious figures have been seen digging feverishly in the woods on dark nights by the lights of tin lanterns. They are the pirate ghosts returning to claim their lost loot.

Another version of this was recorded by Richmond Times-Dispatch staff writer Bill McKelway in 1973. "Some say," he wrote, "Blackbeard, the infamous Edward Teach, intercepted the treasure and then murdered the men who were hiding it. At any rate, legend has it that those murdered men still haunt the woods today, preying on those who dare to trespass the blood-stained earth in search of the lost treasures."

A second possible reason may also have occurred in the second half of the 17th century. After being defeated at the Battle of Worcester in 1651, Charles II of England was said to have considered coming to Virginia. In preparation for his trip, a group of his followers dispatched several chests of money, plate and jewels to the colony by ship. However, for some unexplained reason, the riches never reached Jamestown. Instead, the ship sailed up the Chesapeake Bay and anchored in waters at the mouth of White's Creek near Old House Woods. There, the treasure was offloaded. But before it could be safely hidden, the Royalists were attacked and murdered by a gang of renegade indentured servants. In their rush to escape, these bondsmen took only part of the loot, planning to come back later for the rest. But they, too, ran afoul of the elements. A sudden storm struck the bay and all hands on board drowned when their ship capsized.

It may well be that the storms which took the lives of both the pirates and the renegades account for one of the many Old House Woods ghost stories — that of the "Storm Woman." She has been described by those who claim to have seen her as "a wraith of a woman in a long nightgown, her long, fair hair flying back from her shoulders." Reportedly, whenever black clouds gather over this section of the bay, foretelling a coming gale, her figure rises above the tops of towering pine trees, and she wails loudly to warn watermen and fishermen to take cover.

The third theory about the hauntings supposedly happened in late 1781, just before Lord Cornwallis' army was defeated at Yorktown. Tradition has it that two British officers and four soldiers were entrusted by their superiors with a huge amount of money and treasure. They slipped through enemy lines and headed north, hoping to find a British ship on the Chesapeake Bay. They managed to bury their riches in Old House Woods before they were found and killed by a unit of American cavalry. Thus, it may be their ghosts who still hover over the site in eternal guard.

Whether or not one subscribes to one or more of these reasons, or to none at all, they do offer some possible insight into why certain sights have appeared to a host of people in the area over the years.

And the sightings have been prolific and explicit, however far fetched they may sound today. One of the most celebrated is attributed to Jesse Hudgins, described as a respectable merchant of unquestioned integrity, who ran a store in the town of Mathews Court House in the 1920s. Hudgins told his story to a Baltimore Sun newspaper reporter in 1926, and to anyone else who would listen, and he swore to its authenticity.

"I do not care whether I am believed or not," he often said. "I am not apologetic nor ashamed to say I have seen ghosts (in Old House Woods). I have seen ghosts not once, but a dozen times. I was 17 when I first actually saw a ghost, or spirit. One October night I sat by the lamp reading. A neighbor whose child was very ill came asking me to drive to Mathews for the doctor. We had no telephone in those days. I hitched up and started for town. The night was gusty, clouds drifting now and then over the moon, but I could see perfectly, and whistled as I drove along.

"Nearing Old House itself, I saw a light about 50 yards ahead moving along the road in the direction I was going. My horse, usually afraid of nothing, cowered and trembled violently. I felt rather uneasy myself. I have seen lights on the road at night, shining lanterns carried by men, but this light was different. There was something unearthly about it. The rays seemed to come from nowhere, and yet they moved with the bearer."

Hudgins continued: "I gained on the traveler, and as I stand here before you, what I saw was a big man wearing a suit of armor. Over his shoulder was a gun, the muzzle end of which looked like a fish horn. As he strode, or floated along, he made no noise. My horse stopped still. I was weak with terror and horror. I wasn't 20 feet from the thing, whatever it was, when it, too, stopped and faced me.

"At the same time, the woods about 100 feet from the wayfarer became alive with lights and moving forms. Some carried guns like the one borne by the man or thing in the road, others carried shovels of an outlandish type, while still others dug furiously near a dead pine tree.

"As, my gaze returned to the first shadowy figure, what I saw was not a man in armor, but a skeleton, and every bone of it was visible through the iron of the armor, as though

34

it were made of glass. The skull, which seemed to be illuminated from within, grinned at me horribly. Then, raising aloft a sword, which I had not hitherto noticed, the awful specter started towards me menacingly.

"I could stand no more. Reason left me. When I came to it was broad daylight and I lay upon my bed at home. Members of my family said the horse had run away. They found me at the turn of the road beyond Old House Woods. They thought I had fallen asleep. The best proof that this was not so was we could not even lead Tom (the horse) by the Old House Woods for months afterwards, and to the day he died, whenever he approached the woods, he would tremble violently and cower. It was pitiful to see that fine animal become such a victim of terror."

Hudgins story, strange as it may seem, was corroborated some years later, according to newspaper reports at the time. One account said: "A Richmond youth had tire trouble at a lonely spot along the road near the haunted woods one night, very late. As he knelt in the road a voice behind him asked: 'Is this the king's highway? I've lost my ship.' When the youth turned to look, he beheld a skeleton in armor within a few paces of him. Yelling like a maniac, the frightened motorist ran from the spot in terror and did not return for his car until the next day."

Perhaps the most unusual phenomenon sighted in Old House Woods is the legendary ghost ship. It allegedly has been seen by many, some from a far distance, some from frightening close range. One of the most descriptive accounts was given more than 60 years ago by Ben Ferbee (or Ferebee) a fisherman who lived along the Chesapeake Bay shore early in the 20th century.

His vivid recollection, also told to a newspaper reporter, in 1926, is as follows: "One starry night I was fishing off the mouth of White's Creek well out in the bay. As the flood tide would not set in for some time, I decided to get the good fishing and come home with the early moon. It must have been after midnight when, as I turned to bait up a line in the stern of my boat, I saw a full-rigged ship in the bay, standing pretty well in. I was quite surprised, I tell you. Full-rigged ships were mighty scarce then; besides that, I knew I was in for it if she kept that course. On the ship came, with lights at every masthead and spar, and I was plumb scared.

"They'll run me down and sink me, I thought. I shouted to sailors leaning over her rails forward, but they paid no heed to me. Just as I thought she would strike me, the helmsman put her hard aport and she passed so close that I was almost swamped by the wash. She was a beautiful ship, but different from any I had ever seen. There are no ships like her on any ocean. She made no noise at all, and when she had gone by, the most beautiful harp and organ music I ever heard came back to me.

"The ship sailed right up to the beach and never stopped, but kept right on. Over the sandy beach she swept, floating through the air and up to the Bay Shore road, her keel about 20 feet from the ground. I could still hear the music. But I was scared out of my wits. I knew it was not a real ship. It was a ghost ship!

"Well, sir, I pulled up my anchor and started for home up White's Creek. I could see that ship hanging over Old House Woods, just as though she was anchored in the sea. And running down to the woods was a rope ladder, lined with the forms of men carrying tools and other contraptions.

"When I got home my wife was up, but had no supper for me. Instead, she and the children were praying. I knew what was the matter. Without speaking a word she pointed to Old House Woods, a scared look on her face. She and the children had seen the ship standing over the woods. I didn't need to ask her — I started praying too."

Soon after, Ferbee and his family moved from the area.

Many others claim to have sighted the fabled ghost ship. One was a 14-year-old Mathews County boy who related his experience this way: "A friend of mine and I were taking a boat from Mathews Yacht Club over to Moon post office. You go up Stutts Creek and then over to Billups Creek. It was just after sunset and everything was sort of misty. Then about a half mile from the mouth of the creek, we saw it. We both saw it, but couldn't believe it. I'd never seen anything like it before.

"There was a big sailing ship floating in the marsh. It had two or three masts and was made of wood. There's only a foot of water there but it looked like it was floating. It was the kind of ship the pirates used. We watched for about a

hundred yards more and then it just disappeared. I went home and told my mother, but she just laughed. She said everyone knew of the stories about the ghosts in Old House Woods."

Another who saw the phantom galleon, and many other things too, was Harry Forrest, a farmer-fisherman who lived only 600 yards from the edge of the woods. "I've seen more strange things in there than I could relate in a whole day," he once said before his death in the 1950s. "I've seen armies of marching British redcoats. I've seen the 'Storm Woman' and heard her dismal wailings, and my mother and I have sat here all hours of the night and seen lights in the woods. We have sat here on our porch overlooking Chesapeake Bay and seen ships anchor off the beach and boats put into shore, and forms of men go to the woods. I would see lights over there and hear the sound of digging."

Forrest told of his ship sighting this way: "I was out fishing right off the beach one day in broad daylight when I saw a full-rigged ship headed straight for me, just 100 yards away. I rowed to shore as fast as I could, and just as I got on the beach, she started drifting, and she lifted and sailed straight to the Old House Woods, and you heard the anchor chain clank."

On another occasion, Forrest recalled: "Tom and Jack Diggs and I were going through the woods one night when one of those ships must have been just about to land. There was a terrible racket right close to the Old Cow Hole as she dropped anchor, and then she drifted off with that blaze of light running right along through the hawsepipe. I've seen many a one, and they all go off that way. It's the chain running out too fast through the hawsepipe that starts the blaze. And such bumping you never heard. Most of 'em are square riggers."

The Old Cow Hole, it should be explained, is where Forrest believed treasure was buried. It is somewhere near the center of the woods. He once took a newsman to the sight. The reporter described it as being a "small, circular pool of gray water, which seemed to swirl, and yet it was dead still."

"This is where they buried the money," Forrest told him. "I think they must have killed a pirate and put him with it. There's everything in there. You hear chains rattle sometimes. I've seen everything on earth a man could see in these woods — not so much in the day-time, but it's bad enough then."

While Forrest claimed he was not afraid of the dead, even though he believed the dead come back, one experience he told of even shook him to the marrow. "Once I went out one brilliant November night to shoot black ducks," he recalled. "I found a flock asleep on a little inlet where the pine trees came down to the edge of the water. As I raised my gun to fire, instead of them being ducks, I saw they were soldiers of the olden time. Headed by an officer, company after company of them formed and marched out of the water.

"Recovering from my astonishment and bewilderment, I ran to my skiff, tied up on the other side of the point. Arriving there, I found a man in uniform, his red coat showing brilliantly in the bright moonlight, sitting upright and very rigid in the stern. I was scared, but mad, too. So I yelled to him 'Get out of that skiff or I'll shoot.'

" 'Shoot and the devil's curse to you and your traitor's breed,' he answered, and made as if to strike me with the sword he carried. Then I threw my gun on him and pulled. It didn't go off. I pulled the trigger again. No better result. I dropped the gun and ran for home, and I'm not ashamed to say I swam the creek in doing it, too,"

Forrest also used to tell of seeing a white ox lying in his cornfield one night. "I went out to drive him away," he said. "When I reached the spot where the animal was lying, I saw it was a coffin covered with a sheet and borne along by invisible hands, just at the height pallbearers would carry a corpse. I followed until it entered the woods. The sheet only partly covered the coffin.

"Well, sir, the following Wednesday they brought the body of Harry Daniels ashore from Wolf Trap lightship. Harry was killed when the boiler blew up aboard the lightship. As the men carried him up the beach to the waiting hearse, I recognized instantly the coffin I had seen borne into Old House Woods. The men were carrying it in the selfsame manner in every particular, a somewhat clumsy, swaying motion I had observed in my cornfield."

Still another tale that has been printed in both books and newspapers involved a farmer's wife who lived adjacent to the haunted woods. One evening at dusk she went into a pasture to bring home their work horses. She drove them down a lane towards the barn. Arriving at the gate, she called to her husband to open it. He did not respond at once, and she opened it herself. As she did so, her husband came out of the barn and laughed at her, saying he had put the team in the stable two hours before.

"Don't be foolish," she said. When she turned to let the team pass through the gate, instead of two horses standing there, she saw two headless black dogs scampering off towards Old House Woods! "That woman," says Olivia Davis today, "was my great grandmother." Over the years there also have been numerous reported sightings of headless cattle wandering aimlessly in the woods.

Through the decades there have been many mysterious disappearances in the area, involving both humans and animals. None has been satisfactorily explained to this date. In 1950, Harry Forrest told of one. "It was near about 100 years ago that Lock Owens and Pidge Morgan came through these woods with their steer, on the way back from a cattle auction, and nothing's been seen of 'em since. Steer, carts and everything disappeared in there. Lock had a little black dog and the only thing that ever was found of it was a little bunch of hair off of that dog's tail.

"There used to be a lot of cattle down on these points, but they got to wandering in here and never came out," Forrest said. "Everything that comes in here heads for the Old Cow Hole and disappears. It's very strange. One night that Old Cow Hole will be covered with water, the next it's dry. Some nights it'll be light enough to pick up a pin in these woods, and black and storming outside. And some, you'll come in here and it'll be pouring down. You get wringing, soaking wet, you can wipe the water off you. And then you come out and you'll be perfectly dry."

And finally, there is the tragic tale of Tom Pipkin, a local fisherman who lived in the vicinity around 1880. Fired up by the age-old stories of buried or sunken gold, he took his small boat into the woods, following an old channel some say was originally cut by pirates two centuries earlier, and headed for Old Cow Hole.

Several days later his boat was found in the bay. Inside the boat were two gold coins of unknown age, and a battered silver cup covered with slime and mud. One coin bore a Roman head, and the letters "I V V S" were distinguishable. No one would take Pipkin's boat and it rotted away on nearby Gwynn's Island. He was never heard from again.

"A thousand people have been in here after that money, but they'll never get it," Harry Forrest once said of Old House Woods. "The trees start bending double and howling. It storms. And they get scared and take off . . . The woods is haunted, that's what it is."

Eerie Sounds at Elmwood

f there are any ghosts in the house today, I don't know anything about them," says Mrs. Helene Garnett, mistress of Elmwood, near Tappahannock in Essex County. She should know. Her late husband, who was a direct descendent of the mansion's builder, dating to pre-Revolutionary War days, inherited Elmwood in 1943, and Mrs. Garnett has lived there ever since. Her husband died about 10 years ago.

"Oh, I've read the books and I've heard the stories, but I'm pretty much a down-to-earth person. I don't particularly believe in all that. I have never heard or seen anything out of the ordinary," she says.

But there was a time, swear many long-time county residents, when the great house was indeed haunted by multiple spirits ranging from the fun-loving and jolly, to one who screamed in agony from a horrible accident which befell him more than a century and a half ago.

In fact, there was a time in the 1930s, following the publication in a Fredericksburg newspaper of the ghosts at Elmwood, when the manor, then abandoned, became the focal point of curiosity seekers for miles around. "People came here from all over after that article was published," says Mrs. Garnett. "They would sit on the kitchen steps at midnight waiting for something to happen."

They were drawn like moths to a flame by descriptions of the house such as: "it is isolated from modernity, and no scenic setting could be built more suited to the tales of haunted houses;" and "a sense of isolation without peace, remoteness without tranquility, pervades the air. The silence is oppressive! A weird influence permeates the abandoned structure."

To these solemn accounts, written in the 1930s, were added reports from neighbors and others that strange sounds could be heard emanating from the house late at night; strange because the house had then been deserted for more than

65 years!

Elmwood was built in the mid 1700s by Muscoe Garnett for his son, James Mercer Garnett. The estate comprised 1,000 acres, and the huge house was described as one of the finest in the Colony. Made of brick, it stretched an incredible 100 feet across the front flanked by twin chimneys and adorned with 20 windows, 10 on each floor. The main hall is 20 feet wide, leading to cross halls, each 10 feet wide and 20 feet long. Hall woodwork is elegant black walnut, hand-carved and in natural finish. At the cross hall entrances there are arches that have been called the finest work of Colonial architects.

In the blue room is a rose colored marble mantel, and above it a cornice of soft white and blue, touched with silver. A Victorian book shelf is filled with periodicals and books in French, English, German and Latin. A carved rosewood sofa is at one end of the room and there are chairs of the same soft tint, upholstered in sapphire velvet. By the door stands an old spinet.

Carved woodwork distinguishes the enormous drawing room with paneled walls a delicate ivory color. Like the doors, the wainscot and baseboard are the soft color of the natural black walnut wood. The mantel, ashes-of-roses in color, is made of the finest marble. In the library, paneled with curly maple, are built-in book shelves of maple and mahogany.

In the days of James Mercer Garnett, it was said to be a most hospitable home, often filled with visitors. Many a gay party and dance were held at Elmwood. The house was remodeled in 1850 by the third Muscoe Garnett, who removed the old stairway and added a tower. It was occupied at different times by both Confederate and Federal troops during the Civil War. Then in 1870, the family moved out, and Elmwood stood vacant for the next 70 or more years.

It was during this brooding period that the many ghostly manifestations surfaced. Although the house was empty, the furniture and many antiques and other items remained in it and were watched over by a succession of caretakers. It was these custodians, neighbors, and others who occasionally passed by during the long decades between 1870 and the 1940s, who said the house was haunted.

The spinet was often heard being played by unseen hands, always late at night, and generally when there was a full moon.

And then there was the revelry. The sounds of great parties, laughter and singing, echoed from the house and swept all the way to the caretakers' cottage. Yet, lantern-lit investigations revealed no human source for the nocturnal merry making. Inside, as the caretakers dusted and cleaned periodically, doors would open and shut mysteriously, and although Elmwood was heavily carpeted, loud footsteps would echo along the halls and in certain rooms.

Even more unnerving to those who kept up the interior of the house during its days of vacancy, was the scary neatness of the "Doctor". He had been a friend of the Garnett family who had come to visit for a "few days" sometime late in the 18th century. He stayed more than 50 years! He was accepted as a member of the household, and was known as an entertaining man of "cheerful yesterdays and confident tomorrows". He also was a meticulous tidier who wouldn't allow servants in his room to clean. He kept it spotless himself.

A century after his death caretakers still were afraid to enter his room. He was believed by some to have "come back" to walk softly about at night placing things as he wanted them to be, changing them around when the mood struck him, dusting off the furniture, and leaving the room immaculate, and once again silent, by dawn.

It also has been reported that once when the house was still occupied and in its heyday, likely in the early 1800s, in the midst of a gala ball, as the hour grew late, "a couple long since dead, dressed in the quaint costume of their day, descended the stair, hand in hand, and danced a stately minuet the entire length of the hall! Silent with amazement, the gay revelers drew aside, giving ample space to the ghostly visitors, who leisurely and gracefully danced to the far end and out the door, disappearing in the darkness!"

And, finally, there were the spine-chilling shrieks which pierced Elmwood's grounds on nights when storms of wind, thunder and lightning "bent the pine trees and lashed the house." Neighbors and caretakers told of the screams rising above the roar of the storm; shattering cries of agony. And those aware of the history of the house believed they knew the cause. One of the young Garretts was crushed with his horse by a huge falling tree one night as he rode homeward in a terrible storm. His battered body was found the next morning.

But once the house became occupied again in the 1940s by members of the Garnett family, ending 70-odd years of eerie emptiness, the ghostly sounds ceased. It is as if to say the Elmwood ghosts, outraged at their abandonment for seven decades, could finally rest in peace once they knew their home was back again in friendly hands.

Enigmatic Entities on the Eastern Shore

One has to love the names of the towns on Virginia's historic Eastern Shore. There are the Indian names: Nassawadox; Wachapreague; Occohannock Creek; Onancock; Assateague; and Machipongo, among others. Then there are the others which conjure up all sorts of imaginative thoughts: Temperanceville; Birds Nest; Oyster; Wreck Island; Savage's Neck; and Locustville, to name a few. This long, narrow peninsula is dotted with monuments, blacksmith shops, many houses dating to the 18th and 17th centuries, and a debtors' prison complete with whipping posts. At Eastville, in fact, America's oldest continuous court records are on file — from 1632.

There is rich lore, too, about the swashbuckling pirates who roamed the coastline in bygone days and hid out in the numerous coves, inlets and backwaters of the area, which also served as safe havens for rum runners during prohibition earlier this century.

With such a long and colorful history, it would be natural to assume the Eastern Shore would harbor galaxies of ghost stories, but this is not the case. There are a few, but not nearly as many as one might suspect. "I have only heard of a relative handful, and I can't explain why there aren't more," says L. Floyd Nock, a local historian who wrote "Drummondtown - A One Horse Town," in 1976. It is a splendid history of Accomac Court House, Virginia.

Recounted in the footnotes of Nock's book is what he calls a "ghostly related" anecdote concerning William Robinson Custis, the area's first postmaster and son of a Revolutionary War officer. It occurred in November 1839 and was recounted, decades later, by a slave who had been born in 1855 on a farm next to the Custis property.

According to Nock, the slave told the following story: "Major Bob (Custis) was quite ill and not expected to live. One night, his slaves, who were gathered around the kitchen fireplace, heard a buggy approach the house. Upon looking outside, they were unable to see any vehicle — although the moon was bright. The buggy was heard to pull up in front of the house, stop, and then leave in great haste.

"The next morning, to no one's surprise, 'Marse Bob' was dead. When the slave inquired of the family who had visited late the night before, they were told that no one had come. Curiosity caused them to examine the road, whereupon buggy tracks were found in the sand. Furthermore, the grass had been singed where the wheels had left the driveway and run over grass in the yard, leading the slaves to think they knew who had come to take 'Marse Bob' away in his fiery-wheeled buggy."

* * * * *

One of the more notable edifices in and around the town of Accomac is the Seymour House, which author Nock described in his book as a fine example of the indigenous Eastern Shore of Virginia architectural style: "big house, little house, colonnade and kitchen". It was built in the 1790s for Fenwick Fisher, "doctor of phisick", on two lots on Front Street for 21 pounds and 14 shillings. Additions were made in the early 1800s.

There are many interesting legends surrounding the house. One is that a Mrs. Seymour buried a lot of money in the basement; an enticing rumor which led to the digging up of the basement floor by Union soldiers during the Civil War. Some of the legends involve ghosts, not all of them human. One of the most popular traditions is the "Big Black Dog" story, which, according to Nock, "involves the appearance of a strange black animal on the stairway at the time an elderly aunt, visiting in the house, was ill." For some unexplained reason, a member of the household shot the dog on the fourth step as it climbed to the second floor. Here, says Nock, "the dog immediately disappeared without a trace, and four nights later the elderly lady passed to her reward."

There are, Nock adds, several versions to what is called the "Crying Infant" story, all of which involve the cries of a newborn baby heard late on blustery nights. He describes it as a story of an illegitimate birth and the smothering to death of the infant. "The child," Nock relates, "was the result of a clandestine union between the mother, a member of the family living in the house, or a member of the household staff, and the father who was living across the street at West View. The body or skeleton was found in a second floor closet or under the eaves on the third floor." The incident caused a feud between the two families, and the residents of West View bricked over all the windows in the end of the house facing Seymour House. According to Nock, a moaning, crying noise heard on windy, stormy nights by the present-day residents gives "a touch of credence to the tale."

There also is an "Irate Visitor" story. Nock tells it well: "It is said that a lady who frequently visited overnight once announced at breakfast that she had spent her last night there (in the house) because of the peculiar noise she had heard on the previous night; a man breathing heavily in her bedroom. She interpreted the sound as a visit from a deceased resident rather than a possible romantic intrusion by a living prowler."

CHAPTER 9

The curtain, a funeral

pall, Comes down with

the rush of a storm

(The Conqueror Worm)

The Mystery of the Bloody Millstone

h, she's still around. We still hear from her every once in a while. We find things out of place, you know, where they shouldn't be. And the stain still appears on the stone every time it rains. She's still a part of her family."

Sam Nock is talking about the resident ghost at Warwick, the ancestral home of the Upshur family at the small town of Quinby in Accomack County on the Eastern Shore. Sam is a teacher at Nandua High School there. The ghost is that of Rachel Upshur who died a terrible and tragic death on Christmas Day nearly 250 years ago.

Sam says Rachel married Abel Upshur sometime around 1725, and they had five children. Abel was the grandson of Arthur Upshur, who had arrived on the Eastern Shore as a cabin boy sometime during the first half of the 17th century and rose to become one of the leading citizens in the area. Abel and Rachel moved to Warwick, one of the earliest brick houses still standing in the county, in 1738.

Eleven years later, on a bitter, blustery and rainy winter night, the couple was awakened by a loud commotion in their chicken house. Although he was ill at the time, Abel got up to check on the noise, although Rachel begged him not to go. She told him she had a terrifying nightmare in which a "white-shrouded, grinning skeleton with upraised arms had solemnly warned her not to venture out of the house that evening."

If she did, she would "meet death in some horrible manner!" Abel reassured her that everything was all right, and for her to stay in bed.

But when he didn't return within a reasonable time, she became worried, hastily threw on a coat over her nightgown, and ventured, Sam Nock believes barefooted, outside to find out what had happened. She found Abel standing in the cold and wetness. The chickens were still making a racket, but he had not discovered why. She implored him to get back in the house.

As they walked toward the door, Rachel stepped up on an old millstone that was embedded in the ground at the foot of the steps. As she did, a fox raced out from under the steps and sank its teeth into one of her heels. Blood spurted out on the millstone as she limped inside.

The fox was rabid, and a few days later Rachel contracted hydrophobia. There was no known cure at the time for this horrid ailment which viciously attacks the nervous system causing a victim great pain, suffering and madness. Family members, with no choice but to put her out of her misery, smothered her to death between two feather mattresses. It was Christmas Day 1749. She was buried in the family plot at Warwick.

The old millstone is still there today. It is a solid gray, well-worn stone. Curiously, Nock declares, whenever it rains and the stone gets wet, a large, dark red stain appears on the identical spot where Rachel bled when the fox bit her so many years ago.

Strange Lights in the Night

Most forms of psychic phenomena are quite limited in scope. Generally, whatever the manifestation, be it the sighting of a milky apparition, the sound of muffled footsteps in the attic, or a blood stain that cannot be scrubbed clean — the particular characteristic is experienced only by a relatively few people. In some cases, only one person, usually psychically sensitive, is involved. In old ancestral homes, often just the immediate family members encounter the extraordinary. Only in a few instances are the occurrences seen, heard, smelled, felt or tasted by appreciable numbers of people.

That is why the mysterious light at West Point is such a rare example. Over the past 100 years or so literally thousands of Tidewater residents swear they have witnessed the light that seemingly appears and disappears before their eyes. In fact, this sensation is so well known and so reliable in its recurrences, that, for decades area teenagers considered it a "cool" thing to drive to the site late at night and wait for it to show up. As often as not they were not disappointed. It is a story that has been retold generation to generation with many common threads, but with conflicting accounts as to what the actual source is.

Skeptics scoff that what is seen is marsh gas, which is common in the area near West Point at a crossroads called Cohoke. Others say that many of those who come looking for the light are well fortified with "liquid courage" and are likely to see anything. But the majority of those who have been there don't buy these explanations.

"There is definitely a light there," counters Mac Germain, a mechanic in Hopewell. "I've seen it and I wasn't drunk and it wasn't swamp gas. If it was swamp gas then why would people have seen the light at all times of the year?" he asks.

"I've seen it and it's real," adds Mrs. Thomas Whitmore of West Point. "It was so bright. When it got close to us we got off the railroad tracks real fast, but nothing came by."

Ed Jenkins, a native of Gloucester says, "We used to go up there (Cohoke) when we were teenagers. It was the thing to do. I saw it. It would come closer and closer and would almost get to you, then it would vanish. Was I scared? Absolutely! One time I shot at it with a shotgun and it disappeared. But it always came back."

"I've seen it a hundred times," says John Waggoner, who grew up in Newport News and is now a plant manager in Georgia. "It was just a big old light and it came straight down the tracks, but when it got to you there was nothing there. It used to scare the hell out of the girls I took there. That's what I liked about it."

One person who firmly rules out any spectral source is Lon Dill, a local historian who has written extensively of the area, and is the author of "York River Yesterdays". "Oh, there is something there," he says. "There is a light. I've never seen it, but a friend of mine has and I believe him. But it is some form of luminescence, which can be caused in several ways. Your eyes can fool you at times, especially at night. The best way to see the light is to be young and take your girl friend and a six-pack to the site," Dill chuckles.

Another person who has tried, with some success, to play down the supernatural aspects of the light at West Point is King William County sheriff W. W. Healy. He recalls that in the 1960s and '70s, "It was almost like a state fair down there. People would come by the carload to see it. It got to the point where the road was blocked." Healy has done his best to discourage curiosity seekers. He even dissuaded NBC Television's "Unsolved Mysteries" crew from coming to film the phenomenon. "For the past few years we haven't had too many problems because there has been nothing written about it," he says. "Personally, I'd be scared to go down there at night. I've known people to go down there with shotguns and shoot at anything resembling the light!"

Maggie Wolfe, a reporter for the Virginia Gazette in Williamsburg, tells of the time she and her husband were driving from Richmond to Williamsburg late at night. "We were taking some back roads just to do something different, and when we got near West Point I got the strangest feeling that is hard to describe. It was overpowering, as if we were in the midst of a super strong presence. We were paralleling the railroad tracks and when we looked over, there was this light. It seemed to be following us. And then it was gone. There was no train, no noise, or anything. I'll never forget it. We didn't know the story of the light until we told friends about it later."

Bruce Johnson is a local farmer who grew up in the Cohoke area and still lives there. His father's farm is within a stone's throw of where the light is most often seen. "A lot of people have gone to see it," Bruce says. "I've seen license plates from all over the country. It seems like it's most often sighted on cloudy or rainy, dismal nights. I only saw it once. It was back when I was in high school, and I was driving home alone one night after a football game. I stopped at the tracks and I definitely saw some type of light. It looked to me like some sort of welder's arc. It had a gaseous type glow. It was kind of scary actually. I didn't stay long." Bruce's wife, Kay, saw it once, too. She described it as a "big bright round ball of light".

Most everyone who has seen the light (or lights) is pretty much in agreement as to its method of appearance. It first shows up far off, maybe several hundred yards down the tracks, then, noiselessly, it approaches, glaring ever brighter as it nears, until its frightening closeness scares off viewers. Its relentless journey can only be impeded by the foolhardy actions of those who either try to run it down or shoot at it. This causes its instant disappearance. Also, although many have tried, including a national magazine film crew, no one has successfully photographed the light.

The source of the light, however, remains a mystery, and, to this day, stirs heated arguments. Many who have seen it contend it is a large lantern, carried by a conductor or brakeman, who allegedly lost his head, (literally), in an unspeakable accident and returns to search for it. One might reasonably ask, why does he look only at night? Others who believe the decapitation story say the light is too large and too bright to be a lantern; that it definitely is a train headlight.

But just as many people believe in the "lost train" theory. They have heard that after the battle of Richmond during the Civil War, in 1864, a train was loaded with wounded Confederate soldiers and dispatched to West Point, where they could recuperate or be sent by ship farther south for recovery and regrouping. The train left Richmond amid a soft chorus of moans but never reached its destination.

One person who has tried to trace the origins of the legend is Bill Travers of Hopewell. He has concluded that there might be two lights involved. "Many people I've talked to say they have seen a bust, that is the head and shoulders of a Confederate soldier, but without distinct features," Travers says. "He is carrying a lantern about 10 feet off the ground. And, beyond the soldier, maybe 300 yards or so, is the large headlight of a train."

The train theory was given some support by the experience of Tom Gulbranson of Oceanview and members of his family one night in 1967. Tom is an amateur psychic sleuth who, over the past 20 years or so, has investigated dozens of haunted houses and sites. He had visited the Cohoke location several times and had seen the light on a few of them. This time he was with his mother, father, brother and a friend.

As they drove up and parked at a strategic point, they noticed another car a few hundred feet away, only about three feet off the tracks, parallel to them. Tom got out his camera equipment and set it up and they waited. It was a bitterly cold night and, after a couple of hours of nothing but silence and darkness, they decided to leave. Just as they were packing up, the light appeared.

"This time it was brighter than I had ever seen it," Tom recalls. "It was an intense light and it came closer and closer. As it neared the other parked car, its startled occupants flicked on their headlights, and when that happened, we all clearly saw the outline of a train."

Apparently, whatever mission the ghost train is on, it hasn't yet been fulfilled because stories of the eerie light persist to this day.

* * * * *

Not to be outdone, residents of Suffolk say they have their own light and their own railroad story behind it. This, too, is a legend that has been around for a long time. Its setting is a bleak stretch of tracks, on the outskirts of the Great Dismal Swamp near Jackson Road, a gloomy and deserted lane close to the North Carolina border.

Larry Parker, an insurance agent who grew up in Suffolk, remembers seeing it one night. "It only lasted a few seconds," he says, "but it felt like days. It was right on top of us. It lit up the front of the car and then was gone. It could be a 'will o' the wisp' (a cloud of swamp gas that becomes fluorescent under certain atmospheric conditions). All I know," Parker adds, "is that for sure there is something out there. I've seen it a half dozen times."

Others have said the light sort of "danced" down the track and that from a distance it looked like an old-fashioned lantern.

"It just appeared all of a sudden out of the trees — a big bright light that moved up and down beside the rails," Raleigh Isaacs, Jr., who lives about two miles from the site, told a newspaper reporter doing a story on Halloween haunts. "We watched it once for about an hour before it finally blinked out."

The Suffolk light is most often sighted in the late summer or early fall, and, as with the West Point phenomenon, there are several versions relating to its origin, all concerning a brakeman:

■ He left his home near the swamp one night in a raging storm to flag down a passing freight train while seeking help for his sick child. The engineer failed to see him in the foggy darkness and the brakeman was decapitated by the speeding locomotive.

■ He was struck while bravely straddling the track to warn the engineer of an oak tree felled by the storm.

■ He was a member of the crew of a train that derailed and lost his head when the cars piled on top of one another.

According to Brad Rock, a Suffolk native and a member of the Tidewater Chapter of the National Railway Historical Society, whichever way the story began, the ending is always the same. "The brakeman was doomed to wander the tracks forever, looking for his head," Rock says.

"Wretches! ye loved her for her
wealth and hated her for her
pride, And when she fell in
feeble health, ye blessed her —
that she died!

(Lenore)

The Spectral Return of Miss Evelyn Byrd

(Author's note: When I did initial research for "The Ghosts of Williamsburg nearly a decade ago, I talked to a number of plantation owners and others along historic Route 5, the colonial link between Richmond and Williamsburg. As a result, several of the stories in that book told of ghosts at Sherwood Forest, Westover, Shirley and Edgewood. Somehow, Berkeley was overlooked, so the many psychic manifestations which appear there were included in "The Ghosts of Richmond". Now, is seems, there also is a ghost, in fact a familiar ghost, at Evelynton Plantation on Route 5, adjacent to Westover Church. It is in the form of the "presence" of Miss Evelyn Byrd, who also haunts Westover. Since Evelynton was named for Miss Byrd, and since it is such an interesting site, I am including it in "The Ghosts of Tidewater". While some of the background material on Miss Evelyn may sound familiar to readers of "The Ghosts of Williamsburg", I believe the story merits inclusion here).

* * * *

One thing that sets Evelynton apart from most of the other well-known plantations along Route 5 is its age. It is just a little more than 50 years old. In the 1930s, Duncan Lee, the noted architect responsible for the restoration of Carter's Grove, was commissioned to design a Georgian Revival manor house atop the original

foundation. Constructed of 250 year old brick, it is considered a brilliant interpretation of the style, and has been lovingly restored and furnished with American, English and continental antiques, many of them family heirlooms.

Actually, the present house is the third one to be built on the crest of a ridge which overlooks both the James River and Westover. The first one was an overseer's home and no one is quite sure when it was built. It was there when Edmund Ruffin, Jr., bought the original plantation site of 860 acres at an auction in 1847.

His father, Edmund Ruffin, has been described in an Evelynton brochure as being "one of the South's most colorful figures". He was, certainly, flamboyant, irascible, and a violently outspoken advocate of state's rights and secession. One biographer said he was "fanatical in his hatred of the North, had long predicted war (between the states), preached disunion, handed out pamphlets, and had encouraged ladies' shooting clubs to prepare Southern women to defend themselves during the conflict".

He also was known as an eccentric genius and has been called the father of American agronomy. His early scientific innovations, based on the discovery of marl as a neutralizer for Virginia's highly acidic soil, rescued the state's declining agricultural economy in the early 19th century.

But Ruffin was probably best known for a single feat. Because of his zealous advocacy of Southern supremacy, he was accorded the honor, at age 66, of firing the first shot of the Civil War at Fort Sumter, South Carolina, in 1861; a fact that came back to haunt Evelynton.

A year later the plantation site played a minor, although interesting role that, but for fate, could have had a devastating effect on General George McClellan's Peninsula campaign and may have altered the entire course of the war. It is known as the battle of Evelynton Heights, and occurred on the rainy morning of July 3, 1862, two days after the bloody fight at Malvern Hill a few miles to the west. There, column after column of courageous Confederate infantryman were murderously mowed down by rows of Union artillery placed at a commanding position at the crest of a hill.

Despite his decisive victory, the cautious-to-a-fault McClellan ordered a retreat back to Harrison's Landing at Berkeley Plantation on the James River. There he pitched camp to rest and regroup his fatigued army of 100,000. But, through an oversight, one of the Union flanks — at Evelynton Heights — was left unprotected.

The men of the charismatic Confederate cavalryman, J.E.B. Stuart, took this strategic point and set up a single howitzer. It was all they had. And here, Stuart miscalculated. He had anticipated being joined by thousands of troops under the commands of generals Stonewall Jackson and James Longstreet. But Jackson's men were exhausted and mired in mud and didn't arrive until the next day. Longstreet's army took a wrong turn and was six miles away when Stuart had his lone cannon, and some erratic congreve rockets, fire on McLellan's encampment.

The unexpected shelling caused considerable alarm, but only minimal damage. Stuart's men were soon routed from the heights by superior forces. By the time Jackson arrived on July 4th, the Federal forces were too entrenched to be removed. Some historians have speculated that had Jackson and Longstreet gotten there in time, the entire Army of the Potomac might have been lost, or at the least, heavy casualties, not to mention loss of prestige, might have resulted.

Possibly because of the embarrassment to the Union at

Evelynton Heights, but much more likely because of the Federal hatred of Edmund Ruffin, the house there was burned to the ground and the fields were laced with salt. The plantation lay in ruins for years.

Evelynton originally belonged to William Byrd II of Westover. He had intended to give it to his lovely daughter, Evelyn, when she married, but this was not to be.

Born in 1707, she was a bright child, precocious and high spirited. Her father was one of the most prominent statesmen of his era, and was called the most polished gentleman in Virginia. He was secretary of the colony for years, advisor to the governor, founder of the city of Richmond, wealthy land owner, and country squire.

When Evelyn was 10, he took her to England, and there she flowered into a beautiful young woman with porcelain-white skin, shining chestnut hair, slanting, almost-Oriental blue-green eyes, and an enigmatic, Mona Lisa-like smile. It is told that when she was presented at court at age 16, the King of England remarked: "I am not surprised why our young men are going to Virginia if there are so many pretty Byrds there."

While in London, Evelyn fell deeply in love with a handsome Englishman, believed to be Charles Morduant, the grandson of Lord Peterborough. Her father violently objected to the romance, threatening to disinherit her and saying, "Nay! Besides all that I will avoid the sight of you as a creature detested."

Evelyn returned to Westover in 1726 a broken young woman. The spark of her personality was dampened and she spent long hours by herself, withdrawn, almost reclusive. A number of potential suitors paid her visits over the next few years, but she spurned them all, much to the chagrin of her father. He referred to her as the "antique virgin".

She died before reaching 30. On her tombstone was inscribed the following: "Here in the sleep of peace reposes the body of Evelyn Byrd, daughter of the Honorable William Byrd. The various and excellent endowments of nature: improved and perfected by an accomplished education formed her, for happiness of her friends; for the ornament of her country. Alas Reader! We can detail nothing, however valued, from unrelenting death. Beauty, fortune, or valued honour! So here a proof! And be reminded by this awful tomb that every worldly comfort fleets away. Excepting only, what arises from imitating the virtues of our friends and the contemplation of their happiness. To which, God was pleased to call this Lady on the 13th day of November, 1737, in the 29th year of her age."

Months later, Evelyn's closest friend in life, Anne Harrison of neighboring Berkeley Plantation, was walking through a poplar grove when she felt "a presence". She turned and saw a figure approaching. It was Evelyn. She was "dressed in white, dazzling in ethereal loveliness. She drifted forward a few steps, kissed her hand to the beholder, smiling happily, and vanished."

In the intervening generations, many others have caught fleeting glimpses of Evelyn, among them former Westover owners and guests. In December 1929, for example, a guest of the Richard Cranes, who then owned the plantation, reported seeing the "filmy, nebulous and cloudy figure of a woman, so transparent no features could be distinguished, only the gauzy texture of the woman's form." It seemed, the guest said, "to be floating a little above the lawn."

But of all who have claimed sightings of Evelyn at Westover, no one could offer a reasonable explanation as to why her restless spirit would want to periodically return to a place which apparently caused her so much unhappiness in life. Nor does it explain why she has reappeared, as recently as when this book was going to press, at Evelynton.

"We haven't seen her," says present plantation mistress Lisa Ruffin Harrison, "but I can tell you this. I have heard many stories of oldtimers in the area who claim to have seen her, and the peculiar thing about these reports is that they are all the same. They came from different people at different times, but they apparently all saw the same thing." Mrs. Harrison says that 40 or 50 years ago many long-time area residents used to come onto the property and fish in Herring Creek which leads into the James River.

"They all told of looking back at the house and seeing the silhouette of what they called 'an old fashioned lady' weeping into her handkerchief in an upstairs window," Mrs. Harrison states. She adds that a number of psychics have visited the house and grounds since they have been reopened to the public in 1986. "Several of them said, with no prompting from us, that Evelyn's presence is definitely here. Some sensed it on the stairs, and others felt a strong sensation in the boxwood gardens." She also has been sighted on a high ridge overlooking the river and Westover.

Barbara Rand, who works at the plantation, has had the same experience. "We had a tour recently, and one of the women, who was a psychic, ran up to me and excitedly declared, 'She's here, she's here'," Mrs. Rand said. "The hair on the woman's arm was standing straight up."

Is it possible Evelyn Byrd returns in hopes of spiritually reuniting with her lost lover of more than 250 years ago?

When Evelyn Byrd died, an eloquent obituary notice was placed in the area newspaper, the Virginia Gazette, in the issue of December 9, 1937. It read:

Ever constant to her Friend,
Vigilant in Truth's Defence;
Entertaining to her End,
Life! brimful of Eloquence,
Youth in Person; Age in Sense,
Nature gave her Store immense.
But she's fled, and is no more,
Yonder soars in Fields of Light!
Robbed of all our little Store,
Death! Oh Death! we're ruined quite!

A Colonial Time Warp

he curious details of the "Curse Tree" of Jamestown Island, where the first English settlers landed in 1607, were covered in the book, "The Ghosts of Williamsburg", initially published in 1983. For those who missed it, a brief recap is in order as a prelude to the story that follows.

In the year 1687, a very feisty, headstrong young lady of 17 named Sarah Harrison, fell in love with the worldly and charismatic James Blair, who had a long and distinguished career during colonial times, including a tenure as one of the first presidents of the College of William and Mary. Sarah's parents were dead set against such a union, principally because Blair was nearly twice her age. But Sarah persisted. She broke an engagement with a young man more suitable to her parents and married Blair. Even then her parents tried to have the marriage annulled, but fate intervened. They were struck by lightning and killed one night in their buggy during a terrible thunder storm.

The Blairs lived happily until Sara died, at age 42, in 1713. She was buried in the small cemetery by the old church on Jamestown Island. her husband lived another 30 years, and then he was interred by her side. In time, a sycamore tree sprang up between their two stones, and, over a period of years, literally pushed their tombs apart. A legend evolved that Sarah's parents, unable to separate the lovers in life, were successful after death.

It is with this background in mind that we set the scene for a second ghostly tale on the island. It was experienced by Gerry McDowell and her late husband, Gus, two decades ago. Both Gerry and Gus were "sensitive" to certain psychic phenomena. For example, when Gus was just 17, he saw the apparition of his mother, who had been dead for three weeks, at the foot of his bed folding his clothes. At first he thought it was a dream, but when he got up the next morning, his clothes, which he had thrown on the floor the previous evening, were neatly folded in a pile on the bedspread.

Once Gus, then a riverboat engineer in Ironton, Ohio,

awoke in the middle of the night and told Gerry he had to go down to the river, his boat was on fire. He dressed and left. A few minutes later the phone rang. Gerry answered. It was Gus' employers saying they needed him because the boat was on fire. Another time, Gus dreamed their son, Donald, was in trouble. He and Gerry drove over to the college dormitory where Donald was housed, and found him on the floor in the hallway. He had pneumonia. They rushed him to the hospital.

Afterwards, Gus and Gerry moved to Virginia, where she now works in the library of the Association for Research and Enlightenment in Virginia Beach — the organization built upon the life and work of psychic of Edgar Cayce. They both liked to travel, and often visited area sites in the off season.

It was on such an excursion to Jamestown Island, in 1971, that the "experience" happened. They were there very early on a chilly autumn morning, because, as Gerry says, "we liked to be out when no one was around so we could enjoy the solitude, and Gus liked to feed the animals."

The story is best told in Gerry's own words, as follows: "I can remember it as clearly as if it happened yesterday, although it now has been 20 years. It was real early on a

Sunday morning. About 6 a.m. It was damp and misty. You could see the fog coming off the river. I was listening to one of those audio recordings which told all about the early settlement, when I had the strangest sensation. There was a deathly stillness in the air.

"I turned around and there, coming down a path toward us was a group of about 20 people, men, women and children. They were all dressed in colonial costume. The men wore knickers with either black or white stockings and shoes with buckles. They had on jacket blouses with wide white collars, and very broad brimmed hats. The ladies were wearing long gray or black dresses, with shawls over their shoulders, and bonnets.

"They were very animated. The men and women were talking and laughing, and waving their arms as they walked. The children were running in and out of the group. I thought at first that it might be a troop of actors who were coming to participate in a play or something. I looked at Gus, and he saw them, too. We stood together and watched as they approached us.

"It was then that we realized there was something different. While they seemed to be talking, there was no sound whatsoever. Instead there was only an icy silence. They didn't appear to be ghosts, because I think most ghosts are wispy or transparent, and they weren't. You couldn't see through them. And then we noticed. They were ghosts, because they were not walking on the ground! They were elevated above it by a few inches.

"Gus and I froze. We stood still and didn't say a thing. We felt together that any movement or sound on our part would dissolve them. On they came. They marched right by us without noticing us. It was as if we weren't there. We could have reached out and touched them, but we didn't. They moved past us and walked straight up the path to the church. When we turned to follow them, we could barely believe our eyes. The church had transformed from its present state to how it must have looked in the early 1600s, complete with steeple and all! Gus and I both gasped.

"They opened the door and, one by one, went inside. When the last gentleman entered, he turned and appeared to stare at us. Gus said he had a smile on his face. I didn't see that, but he slammed the door forcefully. Again, there was no sound. We stood there for a few seconds in silence, transfixed. And then the church appeared in its present state again.

"Neither one of us was afraid of ghosts, so we were not really scared. Still, it was minutes before either of us could speak. Then Gus finally said, 'nobody is going to believe this!' I don't know much about such things, but I think now that we had somehow gotten into a time warp for that brief instant. I have heard about such things, although I don't really understand them. But how else can you explain what happened! All I know is that it was a once in a lifetime experience that I will never forget."

CHAPTER 13

Historical Haunts in Williamsburg

(Author's note: In my book "The Ghosts of Williamsburg", first published in 1983, I included a number of the houses in the historic colonial district — Peyton Randolph, George Wythe, Ludwell-Paradise, and, a few miles away, Carter's Grove. Since that time, some additional ghostly tales have surfaced in the Williamsburg area. They are included here.)

* * * * *

The Revisit of Cuthbert Ogle

lthough the history of 18th century Virginia is more than well documented in the Colonial Williamsburg Foundation library, the Swem Library at the College of William and Mary, the state library in Richmond and elsewhere, relatively little is known about a poor, though apparently talented English musician who came to America probably in the late winter or early spring of 1755. His name was Cuthbert Ogle.

It is recorded that on March 28th of that year, he ran an ad in the Virginia Gazette offering his services to teach "Gentlemen and Ladies to play on the Organ, Harpsichord or Spinet; and to instruct those Gentlemen that play on other instruments so as to enable them to play in Concert". He went on to say that he was living at the Nicolson house in Williamsburg, but that "upon having Encouragement", he would be willing to "fix to any Part of the Country".

This could have indicated that he was having a rough time making ends meet, which was true of most musicians of that year. Peter Pelham, for example, the celebrated musician and organist at Bruton Parish Church from the 1750s to the 1790s, subsidized his meager earnings by serving as the town's jailer. There are sketchy, and unconfirmed, notes that suggest Ogle plied the plantation circuit briefly, playing and teaching music to the aristocratic set. And there are accounts that he was brought over to America not only to be the first organist at Bruton Parish, before Pelham, but also to help install the church's initial organ. Some writers have even called him an "outstanding" musician of the mid-18th century.

If indeed he did achieve a measure of fame, it was shortlived, because Cuthbert Ogle died on April 23, 1755, leaving a scant estate worth only 69 pounds including such assorted items as a nightshirt, a spyglass, an old grey coat and two pairs of "breeches," two pairs of spectacles, a plain gold watch, a fiddle and a case, several "musick" books, two "wiggs" and a hair trunk.

The word was that this mysterious musician passed away even before the organ could be assembled in the church. His legacy of a music library, the importance of which is difficult to ascertain, was allegedly passed on to young Pelham.

It is the ghost, or more precisely, the "presence" of Cuthbert Ogle that is felt in the Nicolson House on York Street, according to Cathy Short, who lived there from 1965 to 1980. "We always called him Cuthbert anyway," she says. Robert Nicolson was a tailor and merchant. His house was built around the middle of the 18th century. He took in lodgers for a number of years, and during the Revolutionary War he and his son, William,

provided uniforms to the American army.

"Of course, there are many noises physically associated with old houses," Cathy says, "and we certainly had our share of creaks and rattles and squeaky steps. But beyond this, there was a definite presence in the house. My husband and oldest son never really felt it, but my youngest son, David, and I often did. And it was a male. I can't tell you why I know this. It was an unstated feeling. At times you could just sense there was something there, always on the second floor. David and I would know this without conferring, yet it never bothered either one of us."

Once, Cathy had some friends over and they were playing bridge downstairs. One, the late Lee Epley, went upstairs to the bathroom, and when she came down, she had an astonished look on her face. "Do you know you have a ghost in this house?" she asked. Cathy, concentrating hard on her card game, didn't even look up. "Yeah," she said, matter of factly. "The other women couldn't believe how nonchalant I was," she adds.

On another occasion, Dot Rascoe of Williamsburg was in the house with others for a meeting when Cathy told them the story of Cuthbert. "I was sitting on the couch," Dot recalls, "and I felt something tap me on the shoulder. I though it was the cat, but when I turned around, there was nothing there!" A similar, though less-than-supernatural occurrence happened one night when several college students were at the house. Again, Cathy was talking about the resident ghost, when her cat playfully tapped one of the coeds on the head. She screamed, and Cathy says, "You never saw so many young ladies move so fast."

Once, in the dead of night, Cathy kept hearing scratching sounds. "I thought it might be a rat or a squirrel, but finally I couldn't stand it any longer. I woke my husband and told him there was someone in the room other than us. He turned on the light and looked around, but found nothing. He went back to bed and said, sarcastically, 'it must be Cuthbert.' Just then, inexplicably, the lamp on his bedside table fell to the floor. And it didn't just fall. It ended up all the way across the room, as if someone had thrown it there. After that, my husband thought maybe there was something to our ghost theory after all."

* * * * *

69

Red Eyes Shining
in the Dark

What would your reaction be if, sleeping late at night for the first time in a strange house, you woke up, and, peering straight out of the guest bedroom down the stairway to the ground floor, you saw a pair of red, flickering eyes staring at you? Fright? Horror? Would you scream? Likely. But Shiela Lake only stared back in fascination.

She still remembers the date — November 28, 1981. She and her husband, Dick, who now run a bed and breakfast in Williamsburg, were in town to check out the William and Mary campus for their oldest son. Rather than stay at a motel, they chose to spend the night in the small building behind Peter Hay's rebuilt apothecary shop, which, they felt, had more "atmosphere." After a late dinner at King's Arms Tavern, they sat before the fireplace until about midnight and then retired to the upstairs bedroom.

"You walk right into the bedroom from the stairs," Shiela recalls. "There is a landing halfway up the stairs and a shoulder high window is located there. Dick had fallen asleep, and I had the strangest sensation that I was being watched. I was lying on one side and when I turned over, I looked through the open door down the stairway. I saw these two red spots. At first, I thought it might be a reflection of the fire in the window, but then, as my eyes adjusted, I saw the distinct shape of a man. The red spots were his eyes!

"For some reason I can't explain, I wasn't frightened. Instinctively, I knew somehow that 'he' wouldn't harm me. I turned my head and then looked back again. He was still there. I could see the outline of him from his head down to just above his ankles. He had on a kind of blouse that seemed to billow at his shoulders. His trousers were like knickers coming down to just below his knees, with long white socks under them. He didn't move, except for the flickering lights in his eyes. And his head seemed to be swathed in bandages.

"After awhile, I guess I nodded off," Shiela says. "Then

Sketched by Shiela Lake

I awoke again about 3 a.m., and I had to go to the bathroom. I turned on the night light and looked down the stairs. There was nothing there. Then, when I got back in bed and turned out the light, I looked again, and there he was, the red eyes glowing as before!"

In reading about the history of the area sometime later, Shiela gasped when she read where Peter Hay's shop had burned to the ground in 1756. Despite his head having been wrapped in bandages, Shiela had the impression that the vision she saw that night was that of a black man. Could it have been a servant, injured in the fire, who had come back to see who was sleeping in his quarters?

* * * * *

The Photogenic Spirit of Croaker

upernatural occurrences are rarely documented with physical evidence. Manifestations are generally seen, heard or felt by one or more individuals, but it is highly unusual to record or photograph spiritual visitations. There was one case in the small community of Croaker, northwest of Williamsburg, where a snapshot was taken of a young couple several years ago in which a spectral "intruder" apparently appeared.

"Sandy," (she preferred not to have her real name used) was a senior at William and Mary in the mid-1970s when she and her cousin rented a 125-year-old farmhouse in Croaker, not realizing it was haunted. Almost immediately, they began hearing "heavy, booted" footsteps, just before dawn, walking down a stairway, through the dining room and out the back door, followed by the door slamming. Sandy's cousin, spooked by the happenings, moved out. The manifestations stayed.

When a male friend temporarily moved into an upstairs bedroom where the mystery footsteps sometimes originated, he was strangely afflicted with a series of seizures. Others, too, including Sandy's father and amateur ghostbuster Tom Gulbranson, witnessed the odd noises. "When I checked the house, it was empty," Gulbranson remembers. "I entered the back door, and I heard heavy footsteps in an upstairs room. My brother and I investigated thoroughly. There was no one there."

The convincer came one night when Sandy and visiting friends took some pictures. One was of a couple sitting on a couch in the living room. When she had the photos developed, Sandy gasped. In the one of the couple, an ethereal, wispy white mass appeared above the head of the young man. "That must be my ghost," she joked.

Some weeks later, Sandy's brother visited her and brought along a friend who was a photo interpreter for the Central Intelligence Agency in Washington. She showed him the photo and he asked if he could take it back to examine it in his lab. She agreed.

Some time later he wrote her of his findings. He said the photo had been carefully examined by a team of expert CIA interpreters, and it was their belief that the "thing" in the picture was a "massive living matter, but not human." Further he said the agency's past experience with photos of this nature was that ghosts never show up unless "standing directly behind a male human being. Apparently, whatever energy source they need to make themselves visible is present in necessary quantity in males."

But to Sandy, the letter created as many questions as it answered. If the mass wasn't human, what was it? Where did it come from? If it was a spirit, why was it there? And finally, when Sandy moved out of the old farmhouse, did the presence remain?

* * * * *

The Stage Struck Specter

Every theater of note seems to have, or perhaps should have, a resident ghost, and Phi Beta Kappa Hall on the campus of the College of William and Mary in Williamsburg is no exception. Here, amidst the presentation of plays ranging from modern drama to Shakespeare, occasionally roams a spectral lady who students long ago named "Lucinda." She has been seen and heard, mostly in the lighting booth or around the stage manager's box for at least the past 30 years. For example:

■ Twenty years ago music student Larry Raiken was by himself in the hall late one night practicing on the piano. Finished, he gathered his belongings and started to leave. Suddenly, a female voice materialized and said, "Oh, don't stop." Raikin looked all around only to find he was alone. He searched the entire auditorium, turning on all the lights he could find. When he entered the scene room below the stage, a fuse blew and the door slammed behind him, leaving him in total darkness for about 20 minutes. Terrified, he ran from the building.

■ In 1970, following a concert at Phi Beta Kappa Hall, Raikin and Calvin Remsberg stayed to clean up. Late at night, they decided to improvise an opera with Raikin at the piano. Remsberg let out a cry of alarm as he saw "the figure of a woman dressed in a long black dress and black veil drift from the stage manager's box to the other side of the stage.

■ Student Wayne Aycock opened a door one evening while working in the lowered pit of the theater. As he did, sparks flew. He then heard organ music, and discovered, in a room under the stage, an old pipe organ which hadn't worked for years. It was playing itself!

■ One year during the production of a musical, John Kirkpatrick, while rehearsing a solo dance, stopped abruptly and screamed. Others in the cast ran on stage, and they all looked up at the balcony. There, they collectively saw a nebulous "white-clad figure" walk out the door. Rehearsal was suspended as the students combed the building, but again came up empty.

■ In the late 1960s, Jeff Rockwell and two of his friends, Scott Black and Paul Hildebrand, both of whom claimed some psychic sensitivities, turned out all of the theater's lights one night after a play rehearsal, and sat in the darkness to see if the ghost lady would appear. They were seated on the edge of the stage in front of the lowered pit. Something flew out of the pit towards them, which they later described as a "rush of air, almost transparent, weird and cold." The mass seemed to chase them as they ran across the stage. It brushed past Hildebrand's ear, and he said it smelled like the "odor of dark crypts."

Although considerable research has been done over the years to determine who Lucinda was, and why she reappears at the hall, nothing definite has ever been determined, although there are several theories. During one seance, students tapped out the name L. Battey, and found she had been active in the theater at the college. She had been killed in either a farming or an auto accident.

Another budding actress, who was to wear a wedding gown in a campus play, died shortly before the play opened. The same dress was later used in another production. One night the leading lady was rehearsing a number when she happened to glance out into the auditorium. She saw the dress "sitting there" as if it were watching her!" Some time later, William and Mary police, on a routine nightly check of the hall, were nearly blinded when a spotlight inexplicably beamed directly into their eyes. They made out a figure in the balcony and raced upstairs. There, they found the same wedding dress folded on a chair. Then a strange noise lured them through the halls of the theater for "quite a long time," but always managed to stay ahead of them.

One wonders, whimsically, what Lucinda might do if MacBeth is ever performed in the hall.

The Jealous Barkeep

ittle did Margaret Thompson know what lay ahead of her when she moved into the old medical shop in Yorktown in 1981. After all, she was excited, and justifiably so. She was now to reside in the heart of the town's historic section, and she was within easy walking distance of her office at the National Park Service. She loved her job as a park officer, and everything appeared to be going her way. Margaret, for the moment at least, was at peace with the world.

The serenity lasted only a few months. Then all hell broke loose. "It started with the flowers," the attractive, effervescent Margaret says today. "I love flowers. I had put all kinds of flowers into the house, most of them in glass jars, and I had placed them on the deep window sills. Well, I came home from work one evening, and the flowers, jars and all, were thrown at me. They were literally thrown at me. And there was no one else in the house. Needless to say, it unnerved me. I have a degree in science — biology — so I was looking for a rational explanation. There had to be one. But I couldn't find it.

"That was the first experience I had with the presence that came to be an intimate if not always welcome part of my life for the next four years," Margaret says. Whatever it was, it made itself known in a number of different ways. "I would hear footsteps in the attic late at night, yet I knew no one was there," she adds. "I had a double dead-bolt lock on the front and back doors. There was no way for anyone to get in, yet the footsteps were very distinct. And every time I would search for the source, I found nothing.

"I would leave some lights on when I went to sleep and when I woke up the entire house would be in darkness. The lights had all been turned out. And then there were the cold spots. Usually they were around the fireplace, or by my bed, or in the bathroom. You could move just a few feet, from one spot to another, and the temperature seemed to drop 10 to 20 degrees. Then if you took a few steps to the other side, you would be out of it. It was weird."

Perplexed, Margaret told some co-workers about her

experiences, and some stayed with her in the house. Nothing ever happened while they were there, and they began giving Margaret strange looks. "People kept telling me I was just nervous and imagining things," she remembers. "Hell, I don't have a nervous bone in my body. They began to think I was crazy, so I stopped telling anybody about it."

The occurrences continued. The ghost seemed to be playful at times, and would hide or misplace Margaret's clothes and personal items. She would search for days for things only to find them out in the open in places where they hadn't been before. Once her mother, Elizabeth Thompson of Richmond, came over for a visit. "She always wore a special pair of flat shoes when she drove," Margaret says. "So when she arrived we placed the shoes on the attic steps. A few days later when she was ready to leave, the shoes were gone. We looked everywhere, but we couldn't find them. They had disappeared. She drove back to Richmond and I followed her in my car. When we got there, we walked into the kitchen, and there were her driving shoes, sitting on top of the kitchen table!"

Margaret's mother had two other brushes with the presence while she was visiting her daughter at Yorktown. On one occasion, she clearly heard the sounds of heavy breathing coming from the fireplace area. On another, a camera's flash attachment exploded on a table near the fireplace. Mrs. Thompson couldn't explain such happenings, but she refused to believe they had anything to do with the supernatural.

At times Margaret would see her rocking chair rock by itself. Her kitten would sometimes slap a paw and leap at an imaginary string, as if it was being dangled by an unseen hand. And there were the odors; powerful odors. "There were three distinct ones," Margaret says. One was wintergreen, and one was Resonil, which is an old-time salve used for such things as scraped knees. Margaret described the third smell as that of a musty old vacuum cleaner bag, which she says is a "standard other world odor." These smells would come and go, as if they were directly associated with the ghost.

As time went on, Margaret began to sense that it was a male spirit and "he" was jealous. It seemed that every time she had a date, if he didn't like the date, he would make his displeasure known. Light fuses would blow inexplicably. Keys would be lost. Items of clothing would be missing, and when there was real irritation, dishes would be smashed and the whole house would be torn apart.

"He" particularly didn't like Margaret's square dance partner. "In square dancing you have matching costumes, down to the handkerchief," she explains. "It's a very precise ensemble, and on nights when I was supposed to go dancing, I couldn't find certain parts of the outfit. So I couldn't go on those nights. Usually, the next day they would surface. It was very frustrating."

Even more bothersome were the times when Margaret would come home from a date to find her house ransacked. "Dishes were all over the floor, and it looked like every drawer in the house had been turned upside down and the contents dumped out," she says. "I really got mad. I cussed at 'him.' I told him I was tired of cleaning up after him." It got so bad, she bought a set of plastic dishes. On one or two occasions she even witnessed objects rising off tables and sailing through the air.

Twice, Margaret caught fleeting glimpses of her spirit. Once, she saw a "flash of white" in the kitchen. The other time, on Yorktown Day, she caught the reflection of a man's shoulder in her mirror. He was clothed in white and had a "blousy-type" sleeve reminiscent of Colonial garb. "I thought someone had gotten into the house and I yelled at him to get out," Margaret says. "But when I turned around to face the mirror there was no one there. I was told later that he wouldn't fully materialize in front of me because there was not enough positive kinetic energy. Since I was not a true believer, there were some 'unfavorable vibes' which held him back."

After a period of several months of intermittent occurrences, the combination of curiosity and frustration got to Margaret. If she were going to continue to be haunted, she wanted to know something about who was doing the haunting and why. Friends suggested she contact an area medium who had a reputation for contacting spirits from "the other world". A seance was set up in Margaret's house. The attendees were Margaret, the medium, and two "friendlies," who were described as people with positive vibes which help bring out spirits.

The seance proved both informative and eventful. "We heard pacing in the attic," Margaret recalls. "There were the

Margaret Thompson

sounds of someone going up and down the stairs, and doors being scratched. There was a big-leafed plant in the room and the leaves bent as if they were being blown by a high wind. The place where the medium sat got as cold as ice, although I was sitting just across the room from her and I was hot.

"The medium said the spirit was in the room with us. She said he was a white male of British lineage from a noble family. He was the second or third son, who had been sent to America more than 200 years ago in disgrace. He was in his 30s, over six feet tall and had dark hair and dark eyes and a full beard. He spoke with a French accent, and he had a badly healed duel wound on his right palm. This possibly explained the odors of wintergreen and Resonil."

The medium said his name was Robert Queasly Baker and that he was very romantic and considered himself a poet. She said he worked in Yorktown during the time of the Revolutionary War in a tavern. "That fit perfectly," Margaret says, "because the medical shop where I lived had been built over the foundation of an old tavern of that period."

The woman said Robert had fought in the battle of Yorktown and had later become destitute, fell ill and died from a disease and was buried in an unmarked grave in the pauper's cemetery in Yorktown. "There was a pauper's cemetery just as she described it," Margaret says, "but the medium had been in town for just a week or two, and I am sure she had no way of knowing about it."

The medium went on. The reason Robert was "with" Margaret was the fact that they had been lovers in the 18th century. He had been a barkeep and she had been a bar maid, a wench "of loose morals". He retained a romantic interest in her and was very protective. This explained his jealous rages when she went out on dates.

The medium then talked about the cold spots in the house. This was Robert. Whenever he was present there would be a cold spot, generally by Margaret's bed, in her bathroom, or by the fireplace with which, the woman said, he was somehow associated. At the end of the seance, the medium asked Robert to leave the house, and within minutes there was a sharp slamming of the front door.

Afterwards, Margaret did some detective work. She verified that there had been an old tavern on the site, and that there was a pauper's cemetery on Read Street, now hidden under a paved parking lot. She found the name Robert Queasly Baker in colonial records. His appearance was substantiated some time later by the Yorktown visit of a 300-pound psychic who told her that Robert did indeed have piercing black eyes, with flaming dark red hair and beard, "like that of a Viking". The psychic was in town to investigate a ghost in the Moore House, and nearly died in the effort. While walking up the stairs in the house he collapsed and said he was suffocating, he couldn't breathe. Margaret helped revive him.

After the seance, Robert's activities diminished somewhat, although he still kicked up a fuss when he became upset. For example, in October 1982, Margaret agreed to be interviewed for a newspaper article about her ghost if the writer would not reveal her name or where she lived. When she met the reporter, Margaret told her, "I had a hard time getting out of the house this morning. All the fuses were blowing, my appliances wouldn't work, and my clothes were out of place.

He's not very happy about this story."

On at least two occasions Robert, who Margaret says often travelled with her, was inadvertently left behind when she returned home. Uncomfortable in strange surroundings, he created mild forms of havoc which brought pleas to Margaret to "get him out of here." Once, for example, she visited her mother in Richmond during the year-end holiday season, and then returned home. Hardly had she arrived when her mother, irate, called. Why, she wanted to know, had Margaret stuffed Christmas cookies deep down into the recesses of her sofa?

"You have to understand that nobody goes into my mother's living room unless she is having special guests," Margaret says. "I told her I hadn't been near the room and that I certainly wouldn't cram cookies in the couch. I said it must be Robert. He must have gotten left behind. She nearly panicked. She wanted me to get him out of there, so I yelled through the phone for Robert to leave. Mother told me later that right after she hung up, she heard the front door slam. I guess Robert didn't want to stay where he wasn't wanted."

On the other occasion, Robert got left behind at the volunteer fire station on Hubbard Lane in Williamsburg. Margaret served as an emergency medical technician, certified in CPR, at the station a few years ago, and sometimes, it seemed, Robert went with her. They even "talked" to him through a Ouija board. This particular time, Margaret left the station to go home and the firemen put a big pot of water on the stove to make a batch of spaghetti, only the water wouldn't boil. They called Margaret and she ordered Robert to leave. Within minutes the firemen heard one of their exterior doors slam shut, and simultaneously, the water on the stove began to boil.

As a sidelight, Margaret says that through Robert during an ouija session, the volunteers found out their station was built on or very close to an old Indian graveyard. In fact, Robert told them about one of the Indians, an old squaw named Severette. It was she, the firemen believed, who once left a woman's footprints in the dust of the loft in the station house. That the place had spirits of its own became more certain in Margaret's mind one night when she came in to pull her shift. She found that a Bible had been placed on every bunk in the building, but no one would tell her why.

"I couldn't get anyone to talk," she recalls. "They all were as white as sheets. Something had obviously scared them." Finally, the truth came out. The volunteers had been playing with the ouija board when they "conjured up the Devil." They said they looked at one of the windows, which was set up high off the ground, and they saw the image of Satan himself looking down upon them. That's when they had gotten out the Bibles and that's all Margaret could get out of them. No one wanted to talk any more about it.

As time wore on, Robert's appearances became less frequent. In 1984, Margaret left the National Park Service and moved to Williamsburg. Since then he has not thrown any tantrums. In fact, he has been eerily silent. "I feel he is still there. He's still protecting me," Margaret says. "I know he'll never harm me. Now, he doesn't feel I need him as much."

Recently, Margaret went to another psychic and had more readings. From these she was told that she and Robert actually had been together in three different lifetimes. One in Yorktown, one during Christ's time on earth, and one in ancient Egyptian times. Perhaps that explains why Margaret, when asked the question if she would be relieved if Robert ever left for good, answered, "I'd never believe he was really gone. I've got him for life."

CHAPTER 15

The Revenge of "Dolly Mammy"

In all the annals of ghost stories recorded in the United States over the past 400 years, one of the most famous, and one that has most often been talked and written about is the notorious "Bell Witch" of Tennessee. What sets this case apart is not so much the characteristics of the psychic manifestations involved— although they, too, were probably as intense and as varied as any in memory, including rappings, howlings, thrown objects, pinchings, slappings, chokings, blasphemous curses, and even a poisoning, among other things.

What is so different about the Bell Witch, separating it from most other lore and legend, is that this particular haunting was unquestionably the most thoroughly documented instance of violent psychic activity ever recorded at the time — early in the 19th century. Literally hundreds of people, including many experts and even the soon-to-be seventh President of the United States, Andrew Jackson, bore witness to the sheer havoc this she-devil wreaked over a sustained period of four years.

It began in 1817 in Robertson County, Tennessee, north of Nashville on the farm of John Bell, who had four sons and a 12-year-old daughter named Betsy. One afternoon, John Bell saw perched on a split-rail fence a black bird of monstrous size. It was much larger than either a vulture or a turkey, and seemed to have an unnerving human gaze. As Bell stood transfixed, the great bird unfolded its wings and flapped across the field, casting a shadow over the skeletal corn stalks that chilled his blood. It was as though he had glimpsed, fleetingly, the shadow of death. This was the harbinger of the witch's arrival.

This was followed soon after by eerie scratchings at the doors and windows of Bell house. The children's hair was pulled, and they were pinched and slapped by unseen hands. At first, the Bells tried to keep their troubles secret, but soon word leaked out and first neighbors, and later others from across the state came to witness the frightening phenomena.

For whatever reason, the specter singled out young Betsy in particular. Her brother, William, wrote about the tormenting in his diary as follows: "This vile, heinous, unknown devil, this torturer of human flesh, that preyed upon the fears of people like a ravenous vulture, spared her (Betsy) not, but rather chose her as a shining mark for an exhibition of its wicked stratagem and devilish tortures."

In time, the witch made herself and her purposes known. She was, she said, Kate Batts, the woman who had sold the farm to the Bells. She claimed to have been cheated in the transaction and had returned from the dead to gain revenge.

When she wasn't harassing Betsy, she turned her wrath on John Bell. He became afflicted with acute pains in his mouth. It was, he said, as if his tongue was growing stiff and then swelling so much that he was neither able to eat nor talk for hours on end. He developed horrible facial contortions and uncontrollable tics. The witch cursed him incessantly, calling him vile names and predicting his imminent death. At the same time she continued to taunt Betsy, dragging her across rooms by the hair and slapping her before dozens of terrified witnesses, until her face turned scarlet.

When Andrew Jackson came with an entourage including a psychic consultant, the witch went into such a rage that she drove the expert from the house. John Bell eventually went into a siege of convulsions, and the Bell Witch somehow transformed a doctor's medicine into a murky, toxic potion which caused Bell to lapse into a coma. When he died, and young Betsy's engagement to her childhood sweetheart was broken, four years after the witch had first appeared, the evil spell apparently was broken.

What has all this to do with Tidewater ghosts? There is a striking similarity between the Bell Witch of Tennessee, and the ghost of "Dolly Mammy" Messick who surfaced some years later in the town of Poquoson. It was almost as if Kate Batts had come back in a reincarnated spirit.

Poquoson is located on a palette of land between Seaford and Yorktown to the north and west, and just above Hampton to the south and east. It derives its colorful name from the Algonquin Indian word "pocosin", which means a swamp or dismal place. It is nearly surrounded by water and is adjacent to the Plum Tree Island National Wildlife Refuge. Since Colonial times, Poquoson has been the home of rugged and closely-knit clans of watermen and farmers. Many current families can date their ancestors in the area back hundreds of years.

For generations, area residents owning cattle let their animals roam freely in lush, marshy regions known locally as "the Commons". Such was the case with "Dolly Mammy", a no-nonsense, hard working and well-liked woman, whose tragic story and haunting reappearances have been remembered and recounted from generation to generation.

The problem is, some of the details have gotten mixed up in the retelling, principally whether what happened involved one or both of Dolly Mammy's teenagers. One respected area author says only one was victimized. Many Poquoson old timers, however, including one whose grandparents were

directly connected to the bizarre incidents, say both girls were unwilling participants. Since the latter supposition seems to be the more prevalent one, let's follow it.

There also is considerable confusion as to precisely when the incident occurred. One version says the date was March 5, 1856. Yet, according to Bill Forrest, a local resident who says Dolly was his great aunt, there is a mention in the Poquoson Waterman's Book, an unofficial genealogical guide, which says she died in 1904 at age 42.

Whatever, it is agreed that it was a cold, blustery day laden with heavy dark clouds hovering over the lowlands. Fearing a snowstorm, Dolly decided to go out into the marshlands to bring in her cows, and asked her daughters, Minnie and Lettie Jane, to go with her. Ensconced comfortably before a fire in the farm house, the girls refused. Some say they were afraid to venture out into howling winds and threatening skies. Others say they sassed their mother.

Angrily flinging on a cloak, Dolly turned to her daughters and told them that if anything happened to her she would return to "hant" them for the rest of their lives. With that, she disappeared into the gloom. When she had not come back by dark, a search party of friends and neighbors was hastily organized, and they tramped through the marshes with lanterns, calling her name, but they found nothing.

The next morning, a lone fisherman, easing his boat up Bell's Oyster Gut, a narrow estuary near the woman's home, was startled at the sight of a bare leg sticking up out of the marsh grasses. He went for help, and soon after the body of Dolly Mammy was recovered. She apparently had been sucked into a pocket of quicksand. It appeared that she had struggled desperately for her life, because the rushes and grasses around her body had been pulled up. Her funeral was well attended.

Not long after that, the haunting threat of Dolly Mammy began to be carried out. One day the girls went to visit nearby relations. No sooner had they arrived when ghostly knockings began to echo loudly throughout the house. Suspecting pranksters, a family member grabbed a heavy piece of wood and barred the door.

Incredibly, the bar leaped into the air from its iron fastenings and flew across the room. The knockings, described as "like an iron fist beating on a thin board", continued and grew in intensity, so much so that they were heard a quarter of a mile away by the master of the house. Rushing back home, he found the girls and his family cowering in terror.

While the thunderous knockings, which seemed to follow the girls wherever they went, especially at their house, continued as the main form of spectral manifestation, there were many other incidents as well. "All sorts of things started to happen," says Randolph Rollins, a spry octogenarian and lifelong resident of Poquoson. Rollins' grandfather was a witness to some of the events.

"I can remember him telling me about one night the two girls slept together in a bed and the next morning when they woke up their hair was tightly braided together," he says. "No one could ever explain that." As the months passed, relatives and neighbors spent considerable time at Dolly's house trying to console the distraught daughters. Rollins' grandfather was one of them.

"He told me many a time about being in the house, when a table in the middle of the living room with a lamp on it would start shaking and jumping up and down. Then the lamp would go out and it would be dark, and he could hear the sounds of someone being slapped. When he relit the lamp, the girls would have red marks on their faces with the imprint of a hand. He said that happened a number of times," Rollins says.

Once, witnesses claimed, as the girls lay in deep sleep in their bed, "something" lifted the bed off the floor and shook it. Another time, an unseen hand snatched a Bible from beneath the pillow of one of the girls and flung it against a wall.

As in the case of the Bell Witch of Tennessee, as word of the eerie doings got around, curiosity seekers from all over came to the house. An army officer from nearby Fort Monroe arrived with the intention of debunking the ghost as a myth. He had his men search the house from cellar to attic and then had guards surround it to ward off any tricksters. Yet that evening, as he sat in the parlor, the knockings were so loud they could be heard a half mile away. Then a lamp seemed to lift itself from a table, sail through the room, and land on the mantel. Having seen and heard enough, the bewildered officer wrote in a report, "Whatever causes the disturbance is of supernatural origin."

Rollins reports that once when his grandfather was in the house, two skeptical lawyers showed up. The rappings grew so deafening, normal conversation couldn't be heard and they abruptly fled. And one memorable evening a spirit medium was invited to hold a seance in the home. It was attended by the girls and a large group of people. According to published accounts of the affair, a "shadowy figure" appeared, winding a ball of yarn. As the figure responded to various commands of the medium, the girls fainted. Then the medium said, "If you are the mother of these girls and are connected with these strange rappings, (which were going on simultaneously) speak!" The girls' names were then called out, followed by wild, shrieking laughter. That was enough to clear the room. Everyone except the girls, the medium, and an old Baptist deacon, departed in haste.

This single "appearance" seemed to be the high point of the hauntings. When one of the girls died, the knockings and other phenomena ceased. The mother had made good her threat.

There is a brief epilogue. In the lush marshes and thick grass of the Commons, through which Poquoson cows roamed freely, there is one small patch of land where, curiously, no vegetation has grown since early this century. It is precisely the spot where the body of Dolly Mammy had been found so long ago!

CHAPTER 16

The bodiless airs, a wizard

route, Flit through thy

chamber in and out

(*The sleeper*)

The Celebrity Spirits of Fort Monroe

There are so many ghosts — famous or otherwise — at historic Fort Monroe in Hampton that it's hard to know where to begin. One can almost take his or her pick of a "celebrity specter" and chances are "it" has been sighted at some point over the past 160 years or so. The star-studded list of apparitions who have allegedly appeared at one time or another include Abraham Lincoln, Jefferson Davis, and his wife, Varina, the Marquis de Lafayette, Ulysses S. Grant, Indian Chief Black Hawk, and a budding young author and poet named Edgar Allan Poe.

In fact, the only major notable who either served or visited the Fort and has not returned in spirit form is Robert E. Lee, who as a young lieutenant helped with the engineering and construction of the facility in the 1830s.

But the list of haunts at Fort Monroe is not limited to the well known. There are numerous nameless ones also, including illicit lovers, and a bevy of perky poltergeists who have been accused of such indignities as smacking officers in the face with flying dish towels, and tossing marble laden tables across rooms. There are even reports — serious ones — of a reptilian monster who has been seen stirring in the ancient moat which surrounds the fort.

Dennis Mroczkowski, Director of the Casemate Museum at the Fort, offers a thought about why so many spirits seem to frequent the site. "With the hundreds of thousands of people who have been assigned to the fort," he says, "there's a large population to draw from for ghosts. There have been numerous sightings of strange apparitions and many tend to repeat themselves and become identified in people's minds with the famous people who have been here." He also believes that the dank and dreary corridors and the thick-walled casemates possibly could have lent some inspiration to the later macabre writings of one-time resident Edgar Allan Poe.

The history of the area dates back to the time of the first English settlement in America. The hardy souls aboard the Godspeed, Susan Constant, and Discovery, saw Old Point Comfort, where Fort Monroe is located, in April 1607, at least two weeks before they dropped anchor at Jamestown. A small exploration party even rowed ashore and met with local Indians.

In 1608, Captain John Smith checked the area out and deemed it an excellent site for a fort. Consequently, a year later, Captain John Ratcliffe was dispatched from Jamestown to build an earth work fortification that was called Fort Algernourne. By 1611, it was well stockaded and had a battery of seven heavy guns and a garrison of 40 men. A century later, there were 70 cannons at the fort, and in 1728, a new brick facility was constructed at Old Point Comfort and was renamed Fort George. This structure was completely destroyed by a fierce hurricane in 1749.

The strategic military value of the site was recognized by the French under Admiral Comte de Grasse during the Revolutionary War when his men re-erected a battery there. The War of 1812 demonstrated the need for an adequate American coastal defense, and over the next few years plans were drawn up for an elaborate system of forts running from Maine to Louisiana.

Old Point Comfort was selected as a key post in this chain, and the assignment for building a new fort there was given to Brigadier General Simon Bernard, a famous French military engineer and former aide-de-camp to Emperor Napoleon I. Construction extended over 15 years, from 1819 to 1834, and it was named Fort Monroe after James Monroe, a Virginian, and the fifth President of the United States.

Upon its completion, the fort had an armament of nearly 200 guns which controlled the channel into Hampton Roads and dominated the approach to Washington by way of the

Chesapeake Bay. In fact, it has often been called "the Gibraltar of Chesapeake Bay." It represented the highest development in the art of seacoast defense at a time when masonry works were still resistant to gunfire, and to this day Fort Monroe remains the largest enclosed fortification in the United States. Standing on the tip of Old Point Comfort, a flat sand spit two and a half miles long, which projects southward from the mainland by Mill Creek, the fort was easily defended and difficult to approach.

So impregnable was this bastion, and so ideally located, it was one of the few Union fortifications in the South that was not captured by the Confederates during the Civil War. It was described as an unassailable base for the Union Army and Navy right in the heart of the Confederacy. Thus President Abraham Lincoln had no qualms about visiting the fort in May 1862 to help plan the attack of Norfolk. It was here, too, in April 1864, that General U. S. Grant outlined the campaign strategy that led to the end of the Civil War.

And it was also at Fort Monroe, a year later, that the imprisonment of Jefferson Davis, the President of the Confederate States of America, led, many believe, to one of the first and most famous ghost stories associated with the site. Davis, who had been planning to reestablish the capital of the

Confederacy in Texas with hopes of continuing the war, was captured near Irwinville, Georgia, on May 10, 1865. His devoted wife, Varina, rushed forward when it appeared that a Northern cavalryman was about to shoot down her defiant husband, who also had been accused, inaccurately, of plotting an attempt to assassinate Lincoln.

Davis was taken to Fort Monroe, then the most powerful fort in the country, to prevent escape or rescue attempts. On May 23, 1865, he was placed in solitary confinement in a cell in Casemate No. 2 (a stone walled chamber), creating a painful incident which almost cost him his life and may well have provided the cause for the periodic spectral return of Varina Davis to Fort Monroe during the past century.

A day after his imprisonment, Davis was ordered to be shackled. When a blacksmith knelt down to rivet the ankle irons in place, the angered Davis knocked him to the floor. He sprang to his feet, raised his hammer, and was about to crush the Southerner's skull when the officer of the day, Captain Jerome Titlow, threw himself between the two men. Thereafter, it took four Union soldiers to subdue Davis long enough for the irons to be secured.

The next day, Dr. John J. Craven, chief medical officer at Fort Monroe, examined the prisoner and was shocked at his sickly appearance. He quickly recommended that the shackles be removed and they were a few days later. Meanwhile, the determined Varina fought hard for more humane treatment of her husband, and eventually she and Dr. Craven were successful. Davis was moved to better quarters in Carroll Hall. In May 1866, Varina got permission from President Andrew Johnson to join Davis at the fort, and she brought along their young daughter, Winnie. Jefferson Davis was released from captivity on May 13, 1867, travelled extensively in Europe, and later retired to Beauvoir, a mansion in Biloxi, Mississippi. He died in 1889 at the age of 81 and today is buried in Hollywood Cemetery in Richmond.

It is supposedly the apparition of the iron-willed Varina who has been seen on occasion at the fort, appearing late at night through the second floor window of quarters directly across from the casemate where her husband had been so harshly shackled. A number of residents have reported seeing her. One awoke early one morning to glimpse the figures of both "a plumpish woman and a young girl peering through the window." She got out of bed and walked toward them, but when she reached out to touch the woman's billowing skirt, the figures disappeared.

A wide range of psychic phenomena has been experienced in a splendid old plantation-style house facing the east sallyport that is known as Old Quarters Number One. Manifestations have included the clumping of boots, the rustling of silken skirts, the sounds of distant laughter and the strange shredding of fresh flower petals in mid-winter.

It is here, appropriately enough in the Lincoln Room, where the image of Honest Abe himself has been seen clad in a dressing gown standing by the fireplace appearing to be deep in thought. According to Jane Keane Polonsky and Joan McFarland Drum, who in 1972 published a book on the ghosts of Fort Monroe, other residents of the house have told of seeing Lafayette, Grant and Chief Black Hawk wandering about. All of them stayed at Old Quarters Number One during their lifetimes.

"Ghost Alley", a lane that runs behind a set of quarters long known as the "Tuileries", is the setting for one of the oldest and saddest stories of the supernatural at Fort Monroe. It is here, always under the cloak of darkness, that the fabled "White Lady" has been seen searching for her long lost lover. In the versions that have been handed down for a century and a quarter, she was a beautiful young woman who once lived in a Tuileries unit with a much older husband, a captain, who has been described by authors Polonsky and Drum as being "stodgy and plodding".

Being of a flirtatious nature, she inevitably, and, as it turned out, tragically, attracted the attentions of a dashing younger officer, and their obvious longings for each other soon became apparent to all but the unimaginative captain. And when he left on a trip, the young lovers consummated their relationship. The captain, however, returned unexpectedly early one evening and caught the lovers in bed. In a fit of rage, he shot his wife. And ever since, she has been sighted fleetingly in a luminescent form roaming the dark alley looking for her handsome companion in hopes of rekindling their once-fervent romance.

Undoubtedly the most famous enlisted man ever to serve at Fort Monroe, even if it was only for a brief four months, was a 19-year-old man named Edgar Allan Poe. He arrived

"Ghost Alley"

at Old Point Comfort on December 15, 1828 and almost immediately sought help to get out of the army so he could pursue a career in writing. He was successful, and was discharged at Fort Monroe on April 15, 1829. He is known to have returned to the area once, 20 years later, when he recited some of his now-famous poetry at the old Hygeia Hotel on September 9, 1849, just four weeks before his death in Baltimore.

It is the spectral image of Poe, many have speculated, that was seen during the late 1960s at housing quarters on Bernard Road which, by coincidence, also backs onto Ghost Alley. It was here that a lady tenant of the house heard a mysterious tapping coming from the rear of a downstairs room one night in May 1968. Upon investigation she saw the figure of a man dressed in a white shirt with puffed sleeves, a red vest, and dark pants. She couldn't see his face in the shadows, even when he turned to give her a disdainful look. In an instant, he vanished in a gray mist through a window. Oddly, it was the same window in which the woman's son, a year earlier, had reported seeing a white mist float toward and go out. The shadowy figure was sighted once more in 1969, in a "bent-over, crouching position" moving down a hallway, where he was said to have gone through a closet door without opening the door!

In other parts of Fort Monroe playful and noisy ghosts, sometimes known as poltergeists, have both frightened and amused, but most often bewildered, residents. At the Old Slave Quarters, for example, officers, their wives and children have been subjected to a series of strange shenanigans over the years. Several tenants have found their downstairs furniture rearranged or shoved into the middle of the room overnight with no rational explanation for how it was done. One couple locked their pet cat in the kitchen at night in hopes it would rid the room of mice. Inexplicably, they would find the cat outside at the back door the next day, meowing to get back in.

At a two-story house next to the chapel, occupants found a heavy chest had been moved during the night and fireplace andirons were rearranged. On other occasions footsteps heard in the night ceased each time a light was turned on, drawers seemed to be opened and shut by unseen hands, doors slammed, and loud bangings and hammerings occurred. Even the post commander's quarters has been affected. There, such items as a pedestal cake stand and a Dresden figurine have been discovered broken overnight with no apparent cause.

The stories do abound at Fort Monroe! There is even an instance of a colonel who told of sighting a "monster" swimming about in the moat which encircles the fort. It is 60 to 150 feet wide and eight feet deep at high tide. The colonel said whatever he saw was pretty big. He followed it to an old footbridge where it disappeared.

The thing about all these happenings at the fort, aside from the sheer number of them, is the consistency with which they have been told and retold over the years in most cases by more than one person, and in some cases by many. The other thing is the durability of the incidents. Some are alleged to have occurred decades or even a century or more ago. Others are far more recent. The ghostly episodes continue even to this day.

Workers at the Casemate Museum, which is well worth a tour in itself, tell of the relatively recent visit of the obviously shaken wife of an officer. She had heard of the many ghostly tales at the fort and wanted to share her own unnerving experience. She had been in a bedroom with her two teenagers watching television one night while her husband was in the basement. Before their startled eyes, a bedside table lifted up and flew across the bedroom, smashing into the fireplace shattering the marble top. She and the children screamed, and their dog went wild, pawing at the floor. Oddly, a Waterford crystal lamp that had been on the table remained unscratched.

And finally there was the officer and his wife who were living in the quarters where Robert E. Lee was once housed. The husband was in the kitchen one night when a wet dish cloth sailed across the room and smacked him soundly in the face. He yelled at his wife, asking her why she had done that. She didn't answer. He discovered later she was outside the house at the time.

The playful poltergeists at Fort Monroe apparently were at it again.

CHAPTER 17

A Sampling of Spectral Vignettes

(Author's note: In my book, "The Ghosts of Richmond," published in 1985, I included a chapter titled, "Legends Lost in Time". It covered several short stories, the origins of which were difficult to track down or to document to a satisfactory degree. In doing research for this book, as in the case of the Richmond book, I heard of leads to many interesting tales; snippets of manifestations. But details were lacking. Herewith, then, are a few of the fragmentary Tidewater "legends". They are presented in rough, incomplete form, because, despite their brevity and sketchiness, they are generally entertaining and should be considered part of the area's lore. And, who knows, perhaps some readers will have more clues that may some day unlock the secrets to these antique mysteries.)

* * * * *

The Ghost Coach of Black Swamp

he screams are still heard occasionally. And the spectral outline of the horse-driven carriage, hurtling into oblivion, is briefly glimpsed before it dematerializes! Such is the legend of the mystery of Black Swamp.

According to the most popular versions of this tale, the daughter of Governor Edward Digges was returning home late one night in her carriage, accompanied by her lady-in-waiting, an escort, and the driver. She had been to a party at the Yorktown Inn and was on the way home to Bellfield Plantation, travelling along the Old Williamsburg Road in York County, which some historians say is the oldest road in the country. George Washington used it on his way to the final surrender in Yorktown.

As the horses galloped through land which is now part of the Naval Weapons Station, something frightened them in the woods and they raced off, out of control, plowing head-long into a quagmire called the Black Swamp. The riders' terrified screams were muffled, as the dark, muddy quicksand swallowed them all, including the coach, without leaving a trace.

Although the Weapons Station officially denies it, there have been persistent stories of military men hearing the screams recurring in that murky area, and catching fleeting glances of the ill-fated coach sinking. In fact, the reports go back to the 1920s, when mention of the sightings was made in the Navy Mine Depot's official log.

In more recent years, a government spokesperson did tell a newspaper reporter that although he had not personally experienced the phenomenon, and there was no physical evidence to support it, that "there have been so many reports, some of them must be true." And if young Miss Digges, her lady-in-waiting, the escort and the driver did not vanish in Black Swamp on that fateful night many years ago, the key question remains unanswered: what did happen to them?

The Friendly Spirit at Longview

ongview, a 200-year-old house in Virginia Beach across from the old Princess Anne Courthouse, is said to be haunted by the spirit of a young Confederate soldier who was severely wounded in the head at the Battle of New Market. The structure, built around 1792, still has most of the its original wide-pegged flooring, doors and hinges.

Emily Buffington, who lived in Longview for 30 years with her husband, Jay, says the ghost is James Howard Whitehurst, who had been a cadet at Virginia Military Institute before taking up arms. He spent the final years of his life with relatives at the house. Mrs. Buffington said manifestations included doors opening and shutting by themselves, all lights going out at the same time although they were on different circuits, and the bell pull in the dining room blowing completely off the wall. "We certainly had enough experiences to convince us," she said. "But it was always a friendly ghost."

* * * * *

The Case of the Disturbed Portrait

t all began in the late 1970s, when Mrs. Herbert Underwood of Suffolk consented to paint the portrait of a young boy who had recently died in a drowning accident. That very night, the family heard a strange knocking noise and the sound of a chair being dragged across the floor of their home on Cedar Street. As the painting progressed, the noises got louder.

Mrs. Underwood's daughter, Sherry, was alone in the house one night when she heard mysterious footsteps on the second story. "I was scared to death," she recalled. She called the police and they searched the house to no avail. All the while, during this period, the family dog howled through the night at unseen intruders.

Finally, when the portrait was finished, Mrs. Underwood tried to photograph it with a Polaroid camera, but each snapshot seemed ruined by what she described as a "hazy ring around the boy's head, like a halo." That night the noises were particularly loud, but once the boy's mother picked up the portrait, the sounds stopped abruptly. He finally was back home.

* * * * *

The House of Tragedy

The exact location of this house has been lost to memory, and attempts to track down the one-time residents who occupied it a number of years ago proved unsuccessful. Still, some of the highlights of the bizarre incidents which occurred there were recalled more than a decade ago in a roundup newspaper article of area ghost tales.

The house was in Newport News, somewhere off Main Street. It was a two-story Cape Cod, and it already had a grim history when a father and his young son moved in. They got a bargain because there had been a recent double murder and a suicide at the site. Soon, they knew they were not alone.

The first "incident" was mild enough. Lights in the house were inexplicably turned on after the father and son had retired for the evening. Then the manifestations progressed. One night the father heard his son walk past his bedroom door down the hall to the bathroom. Then he heard the boy throw up, followed by the toilet being flushed. He grabbed his robe to check, but found his son sound asleep in his bed, and in the bathroom the commode was not running. All was silent.

Next, some time later, came a scene straight out of the movie, "The Exorcist". On this night the father heard his son screaming hysterically. He ran to his room and saw him bouncing and jerking on the bed as if being shaken by some strong, invisible force. As he tried, desperately, to control the seizure, he turned and saw, at the foot of the boy's bed, the apparition of an old woman shrouded in a black hood. When she disappeared a few seconds later, his son's spasms stopped.

On other occasions both father and son heard "murmuring

voices" in the upstairs room where they had stored items left behind by the murder and suicide victims. Other apparitions were seen, too. One was of a beautiful young blonde dressed in 1940s-style tennis attire. The other, which appeared to the father, was a black cat with a rat's body sitting at the foot of his bed. When he kicked at it, it vanished.

There is one postscript. Some time after the father and son had moved out of the house, an amateur ghost busting team got permission from the realtor to spend the night there. They set up cameras, infrared equipment and tape recorders, but after four hours of silence in the shivering, bitter cold, they decided to pack up and go home. Just as they were leaving, they heard footsteps scamper out of an upstairs bathroom, scurry down the hall and enter a bedroom. Then they heard the door slam. They went upstairs to check, but found nothing.

* * * * *

The Siren-Loving Fireman

Of the bells, bells, bells — Bells,
bells, bells — To the moaning
and the groaning of the bells

(*The Bells*)

hey say it is the spirit of young Ben Bishop which opens and shuts doors, sets sirens screaming in the night, and sounds alarms at the Chesapeake Beach Volunteer Fire and Rescue station. Bishop was a deeply dedicated 24-year-old firefighter who died tragically in a vehicular accident near Scranton, Pennsylvania, in 1971. They brought him back to Virginia and his casket was carried to a Norfolk cemetery on his favorite fire truck.

"Almost immediately after Ben died some of the strangest things began to happen around the station," says Jack Fay, former president of the volunteers. "The siren on a truck would fire off in the bay with no one around it. I'm not a superstitious man, but it's hard to explain. I have seen a door of a fire truck

101

open with no one in the truck and I saw it shut all by itself. I know that firemen are supposed to be prankish, but I could find no evidence of trickery."

Fay said Ben loved to race down the road with his siren wide open. "That siren still sounds. I didn't know that fire sirens would scream with both switches cut off. But here they do!"

* * * * *

The Phantom Overseer of Suffolk

Suffolk painting contractor W. F. Thompson is used to people looking over his shoulder when he works. After all, isn't every homeowner a painting expert, especially when it comes to his or her house? But as experienced as he is with human nature, even Thompson wasn't prepared for the spectral encounter that occurred a few years ago when he was painting a Suffolk home.

At first, there was the humming. "Several times I heard a woman humming," Thompson said. "I'd hear the song, get down from my ladder and try to see where it was coming from. I knew there was nobody at home. I looked out on the street. There was nobody close by. It sounded as though it was coming from upstairs. It was clearly a woman humming softly to herself, like someone might while doing housework."

But that proved to be just a prelude. One day, Thompson was alone at the house, painting on a ladder in an upstairs guest room. The house was deathly quiet. Then there was a sudden and distinct odor or cigar smoke. "I remember turning around and thinking the man who owned the house had come home," the painter said. "I never remembered him smoking a cigar, but I didn't think anything of it."

Thompson continued to work for several minutes, and then he heard the sound of footsteps approaching the room. They were coming from the short flight of stairs to the guest room. "I had the sensation of somebody watching me," he said. "When I turned around and looked, there was this unique little

102

gentleman. He was wearing a waistcoat, knee britches and stockings. He was just standing there looking at me, his hands on his hips. Before I could move, he turned around and walked out of the room."

Thompson said that as the man left the room he uttered an unmistakable "Humph!", as if he were not satisfied with the workmanship. "It looked as real as though I were looking at a living person," the painter added. "He wasn't transparent. I could see the colors of his clothing and everything. I didn't recognize the man as far as knowing him, but to be dressed that way, I knew immediately he was from another time!"

Thompson said when he told the owners of the house about the incident they didn't even act surprised.

CHAPTER 18

Some Ghosts that Should Have Been

he Tidewater area teems with ghosts and all sorts of paranormal phenomena. Nevertheless, it is surprising to note that, given their place in history, many sites one would assume to be frequented by spirits, are psychically barren instead. One wonders why. In numerous other locations, there are hints of wisps of haunting tales, all too vaporous to track down. If there once were legends associated with these places, they have been lost in time. Still, there is interest enough to mention them in passing.

Why for example, are there no ghosts at Wolstenholme, where a small but flourishing band of hearty settlers formed a town early in the 17th century? Building foundations and various artifacts have been found here at a point between Carter's Grove plantation and the James River near Williamsburg. The townspeople were slaughtered en masse during the savage Indian massacres of 1622. For that matter, why are there no ghosts of scalped and tomahawked colonists up and down the James River, all victims of that infamous uprising?

While there are a couple of Colonial Williamsburg houses included in this collection (and several others such as the Wythe House, the Ludwell-Paradise House and the Peyton-Randolph House were covered in an earlier publication), certainly it should arouse some curiosity as to why there aren't more haunts in the historic area. After all, Thomas Jefferson, George Washington and a great number of other famous and influential patriots spent many a night in the town. Surely, the old Raleigh Tavern and other watering spots must harbor some dark shadows of the past.

There were scattered references here and there: footsteps have been heard in the Norton Cole House; a file cabinet occasionally shakes and a glass ashtray once split in half in the Travis House; and one historical interpreter swears a "violent force" once tried to shove her down the stairs at the Palace. At a house at 22 Nassau Street, two local women had rather unnerving experiences during a visit. One was shoved forward in the dining room while the other said someone or something "grabbed her skirt." Strangely, too, both of their watches stopped while they were in the house. But details and origins of the occurrences proved too sketchy to follow up on.

Speaking of taverns, at Sewell's Ordinary on Route 17 near Gloucester, a restaurant which is open to the public only intermittently, former waitpersons and kitchen help used to whisper about the shenanigans of "Joseph", who allegedly died in an upstairs room eons ago. It is said he liked to change the silverware around and take things away from table settings, but that's as far as the story goes.

Oddly, there are no tales of specters throughout the quaint and colorful community of Guinea, east of Gloucester Point. One would assume given the origins and traditions of this concentration of watermen and their families, all close-knit, that folklorian tales would thrive. But a number of residents who have lived there all their lives couldn't come up with a single encounter. The same was true at Tangier Island and in Urbanna. Such a shame!

There was one account of an ill-fated chap who fell out of a wagon and was killed when one of the wagon wheels decapitated him and his head rolled into Spirit Branch at Gwynn's Island on the Chesapeake Bay north of Mathews. Rumors were the water in the creek has run red ever since.

In the mid-summer of 1862, one of the bloodiest battles of the Civil War took place at Malvern Hill, a short distance off of Route 5 halfway between Richmond and Williamsburg. Here, courageous Confederate soldiers were mown down like hay while attacking the well-fortified artillery position of General George McClellan's men. Hundreds of infantrymen lay wounded, moaning and dying on the long, open hill for days afterward, but there are no reports of any haunting remains there. The same is generally true at other Civil War and Revolutionary War battlefields throughout the area.

Why are there no prevailing stories of ghost sailors stalking the beaches and warning of advancing hurricanes? There is no shortage of tragic shipwrecks off the Tidewater coast. Nor are there any spectral legends about the many pirates who roamed the Chesapeake Bay striking fear into the hearts of seamen for hundreds of miles along the east coast.

It is therefore most disappointing that there is no menacing ghost of the most fabled buccaneer of them all, Edward Teach, the notorious Blackbeard. And well there should be, considering the traumatic events surrounding his life and death. After years of plundering everything in sight, Blackbeard finally met his match in November 1718 at Ocracoke Inlet off the North Carolina Outer Banks. He and his band of cutthroats attacked a ship commanded by Lt. Robert Maynard who had been dispatched by Governor Alexander Spotswood of the Virginia Colony to track the pirate down.

Greatly outnumbered, Blackbeard and his men still waged a furious battle. The pirate chief himself fought as if he were possessed by a demon. Here's how Donald Shomette, author of the authorative book, "Pirates on the Chesapeake," described the action: "Time after time he was struck, spewing blood and roaring imprecations as he stood his ground and fought with great fury. One mighty arm swung his cutlass like a deadly windmill, while the other fired shot after shot from the brace of pistols in his bandolier. The sea about the sloop became literally tinctured with blood. Then, suddenly, while cocking his pistol, Blackbeard the Pirate fell dead, having suffered 25 cut wounds and five pistol shots."

It is what happened next that gives one pause as to wonder why the crusty Edward Teach has never returned to haunt his tormentors. After the fight was over, his head was cut off and placed on the bowsprit of his ship. And there is a legend that his headless body swam seven times around his ship and then sank from sight. Maynard and his crew then sailed back to Virginia. Thirteen of the captured pirates were tried, found guilty and hanged from trees on Capitol Landing Road in Williamsburg.

Blackbeard's head, it is said, was later transferred from the bowsprit of Maynard's ship and placed upon the top of a pole at the mouth of Hampton River, near Kecoughtan. Here, it served for years as a warning to mariners. And, according to author Shomette, it was eventually fashioned into an enormous drinking cup that is believed to still exist.

It's a good story even if no ghost is involved.

Scarce Phenomena in Smithfield

racking down ghost legends in and around Isle of Wight County and the colorful old town of Smithfield, one would think, would be a relatively easy venture. After all, the area is steeped in history and studded with ancient buildings. The venerable Smithfield Inn dates to 1752; the courthouse to 1750; the old jail to 1799; and the Grove to 1790. Stately Victorian mansions adorn Main Street, and then there is the Gingerbread Cottage on Grace Street, and Windsor Castle on Jericho Road. There, too, are cemeteries filled with Civil War veterans, deep piney woods, misty swamps, and shadowy bogs — all key sites often associated with spectral phenomena.

But, oddly, eerie tales of the beyond in this area are few and far between. Many elderly people of the region had difficulty coming up with even a single story, and it took a considerable amount of digging to uncover the following two accounts.

One is told by Mrs. Thelma Edwards, a long time resident. It concerns an old brick building located in the Mill's Swamp region near Route 621 in the northwest part of the county. "That house was haunted, there's no doubt about that," she says. "Everyone up there knew about it, even if some wouldn't talk about it."

According to Mrs. Edwards, years ago some loggers from Courtland were working in the Mill's swamp area, near the Black Water River, for several days. One night, instead of driving all the way back to Courtland, they decided to spend the night in the old brick building. They had heard strange things about the abandoned house, but were tired, and shrugged them off.

Shortly after dinner, as they prepared to go to bed, all hell broke loose. The men heard noises of chains rattling and doors slamming. Then, apparently, the loggers saw the shape of a man with heavy chains hanging from him. That was enough for two of the men. They ran from the house without bothering to pick up their clothes. The third logger, however, stayed, saying he wasn't afraid of anything, and he wasn't about to leave the building and go out in the cold night because of "some noises".

About two in the morning, Mrs. Edwards says, the ghostly man in chains came back with two or three fellow apparitions. The terrified logger then raced from the house and through the woods wearing only his night shirt. The next day the three loggers returned to the old brick house to retrieve their clothes. They were gone and were never found. Nor was any explanation ever discovered for the origins of the ghost bound in chains or his friends.

The second story about Isle of Wight County is better authenticated. It was experienced and is told by Jean Marshall, organist at the Methodist Church. Mrs. Marshall never believed in ghosts. Now she does. Some time ago, for about 10 years, she and her family lived in a county farm house with interesting origins. She believes the house was one of the oldest in the county.

"It is my understanding that during the Civil War there was a path leading through the back woods to the water, and that soldiers docked their boats and came up to the house for various reasons," she says. "Someone said at one time the house was used to hide soldiers during the war." There was, she was told, a hiding place over the kitchen where troops entered through a trap door and went into a small bedroom over the living room.

After living there for about three years, Mrs. Marshall recalls the following, as if it occurred only yesterday. "One night I was asleep alone in the bedroom on the ground floor. I always kept the door locked because the room was separated from the rest of the house by a large hallway and it just made me feel more secure. I was awakened quite suddenly by a hand touching my arm. I followed the arm with my free arm and felt a human body standing beside my bed. It was that of a man, small and young.

"Of course, I was frightened. I turned on the light, checked the door. It was locked. I looked in the closet, under the bed, and under the front porch. There was no one there. I dismissed it as a bad dream and went back to sleep. Then, after several months, 'he' reappeared. But this time my husband was home so I was not alone."

On this occasion, Mrs. Marshall says that sometime during the night she felt something drop on the bottom of the bed. "My first thought was that a mouse had gotten up under the bedspread. it kept moving up the bed, and as it did I was waking up. All of a sudden a gloved hand appeared and moved toward my hand and gently tugged like it wanted me to come with it.

"Now I was fully awake, and standing beside my bed was a young man dressed in a hat, white shirt, gloves, which were leather, a buckled belt and dark pants. He had light hair and wore glasses, and he was smiling at me. Then he was gone." The next morning, Mrs. Marshall drew a picture of him and said he looked like a Civil War soldier. She showed the picture to some friends, but said they just laughed at her. One friend who believed in ghosts, however, offered a possible explanation. She said maybe the young man had been a soldier who had once frequented the room and his returning was some type of anniversary.

Mrs. Marshall said the young man came back once more. This time she did what someone had told her to do on such an occasion. She spoke out loud to him and asked him to leave her alone. That was the last she ever heard of or saw him.

* * * * *

While there is no authentic, documented ghost associated with historic St. Luke's church, just off route 10, four miles east of Smithfield, there is a rather colorful tale that has been circulated for generations. At any rate, it provides an opportunity to give a little background on the church, which is interesting in itself.

Described as an "ancient and beautiful Gothic edifice." St. Luke's was built in 1632 under the supervision of Joseph Bridger, and is the oldest brick Protestant church in America. Traditionally called "Old Brick Church", it originally was in Warrosquyoake Parish, which was divided several times between 1642 and 1752, when it became Newport Parish.

According to local legend, inhabitants of the area during the Revolutionary War buried the county records and the vestry books in an old trunk when they heard of an intended raid by British troops under Tarleton. Unfortunately, after the war when the trunk was dug up, many of the records crumbled to pieces.

The church was not used and remained in neglect from 1830 until the 1890s when it was restored. There is reason enough to suspect a haunting story or two involving St. Luke's Church. Buried, for example, in the adjoining graveyard, are the remains of many Civil War casualties, and there have been a few residents who claim thy have heard moans and cries emanating from the plots late at night. These suppositions are largely unsubstantiated, however.

The one legend that has survived through the ages comes in two different versions. Mrs. H. D. DeShiell, a spry octogenarian who wrote a book on the history of Smithfield, and numerous articles on the region for area newspapers, gives one account.

Exactly when this episode occurred is not known, although it was likely to have been late in the 18th century or early in the 19th, because it involved a rider on horseback at a time, as Mrs. DeShiell puts it "when people still rode horses." Whenever, in those days, the church was in sad disrepair,

virtually in ruins, long before its restoration.

Most of the roof was gone. Nevertheless, it still offered a semblance of shelter on the storm-tossed night a horseback rider approached it. No sooner had he tied his horse, and propped himself up against a wall in a dry corner of the church, when something in the graveyard caught his eye. He described it as a "white, fluttering" sensation. Whatever it was, blurred by the rain and diminished in the darkness, it appeared to be trying to escape an open grave site. Whatever it was, the rider had seen enough. He and his steed galloped away toward town at thoroughbred speed.

The mystery was solved soon afterward, however, with a logical explanation. Either the terrified rider, or someone else, came back in the light of day to investigate. What they found was a rather large goose, which had fallen into the open grave and couldn't quite manage an escape on its own, explaining the frantic fluttering.

What it didn't explain, however, was the repeated sighting over the years around the turn of the 20th century, of a wispy white apparition which many people claimed to have seen, always late at night, in the church cemetery. With each sighting the legend grew of a ghostly woman who allegedly "floated" among the tombstones.

In those bygone days, before sophisticated camera equipment, electronic devices, and professional ghost busters, no one ventured close enough to document details. After all, when travelling at night, especially if you are alone, passing a graveyard is scary enough. And if there is a haunting presence moving about, that is surely reason enough to continue moving on at an accelerated pace.

But this was not true in the case of Dr. "Sandy" Galt, a well known and respected surgeon of his day. He was, at the time, a crusty, fiery old man who knew no fear. He had, after all, operated on wounded Confederate veterans in open fields under constant shelling from the enemy. He had seen the darkest sides of life during his 50 years as a doctor.

And so, when he, too, sought shelter during a storm at the church as he was riding home from Carrollton one evening, he didn't give a second thought to ghosts. And then "she" appeared. In a flash of lightning, he saw a whitish figure flitting about the graveyard. Curiosity, not fear, motivated him to get a closer look, and the myth was unmasked.

The apparition was, in reality, a deranged woman, who delighted in dancing about the old church in the dark, dressed in a flowing white night gown.

CHAPTER 20

Bacon's Castle
Revisited

(Author's note: In 1983, when the first edition of my book, "The Ghosts of Williamsburg and Nearby Environs," was published, I reported an account of the mysterious psychic phenomena, including the sensational "fireball," associated with historic Bacon's Castle in Surry County, northwest of Smithfield. Since that time several accounts of "fresh" manifestations have been told to me, and have been published in newspapers, magazines and books. So many, in fact, that I felt it well worthwhile to revisit the castle and update and expand the chapter to include much of the "new" material for "The Ghosts of Tidewater".)

It was, to the Virginia colonists, an ominous sign of impending disaster. It occurred sometime during "the latter months" of the year 1675. A great comet appeared in the sky sweeping across the heavens trailing a bright orange tail of fire. Soon after this eerie phenomenon came the flight of tens of thousands of passenger pigeons. For days they blanketed the sky, blotting out the sun. Then, in the spring of 1676 a plague of locusts ravaged the colony, devouring every plant in sight and stripping trees of their budding leaves.

But to the colonists, the comet was the worst sign. Many remembered that another comet had streaked across the horizon just before the terrible Indian massacre of 1644. Thus, it was no real surprise to them — because they believed in such spectral omens — when, the following year, one of the bloodiest and most notorious chapters of Virginia History was written.

It began on a quiet summer Sunday when some colonists passing by the Stafford County plantation of Thomas Mathew on their way to church discovered the overseer, Robert Hen, lying in a pool of blood. Nearby lay an Indian servant, dead. Hen also was mortally wounded, but before he expired he managed to gasp, "Doegs! Doegs!" The words struck fear in the hearts of the passersby, for Hen had mentioned the name of a tribe of Indians known for their fierce attacks on white men and women.

The Doeg raid was in retaliation for the killing of several Indians by planters who had caught them stealing pigs and other livestock. Such raids were not new to the colonists. They had been periodically besieged ever since they first landed at Jamestown in 1607. But this latest episode proved to be the last straw with many settlers. For years they had seethed for action by the aristocratic governor of the colonies at the time, Sir William Berkeley, but he was reluctant to move.

And so the seeds had been sown for what was to lead to the largest and most violent insurrection of the colonial era up to that time — Bacon's Rebellion.

Dashing Nathanial Bacon — 28 years old — had arrived in the colony only three years earlier. Well educated and well endowed, he has been described by biographers as "a slender, attractive, dark-haired young man with an impetuous, sometimes fiery temperament and a persuasive tongue." But perhaps above all else, Bacon was a natural leader of men.

While Governor Berkeley remained inactive and inattentive in Jamestown, planters sought out Bacon to lead retaliatory strikes against the marauding Indians. When his own plantation was attacked and his overseer killed, Bacon agreed. He proved to be a skilled and capable military commander. On one march his forces drove the Pamunkey tribe deep into Dragon's Swamp. Later, Bacon overpowered the Susquehannocks, killing "at least 100 Indians", and capturing others.

Berkeley, furious at the unauthorized attacks launched by this rebellious group, dispatched his own troops to capture Bacon and his men. For the next several weeks the two men waged a cat-and-mouse game that involved daring, intrigue and bloodshed.

At one point Bacon surrendered, was brought before Berkeley and was forgiven when he repented. But then he escaped, returned with a force of 600 men and captured Jamestown, demanding a commission to fight the Indians, as well as the repeal of some harsh colonial laws. With no other choice under the show of arms, Berkeley granted the wishes, but when Bacon set out again chasing Indians, the Governor repudiated all agreements and sent his troops after the rebels.

After several skirmishes, Bacon recaptured Jamestown and had it sacked and burned to the ground. Berkeley, who had retreated to the Eastern Shore of Virginia, meanwhile, was regrouping his forces for a final and decisive confrontation. It never came to pass.

Bacon, who had suffered an attack of malaria at Jamestown, fell critically ill in Gloucester and died of dysentery there on October 26, 1676, at the age of 29. With the leader lost, the rebellion fell apart and Berkeley's forces captured many of Bacon's men. A large number of them were hanged, continuing for several more months, the tragedy forewarned by the appearance of the comet.

For three months in 1676 about 70 of Bacon's followers occupied a large brick mansion in Surry County, just across the James River from Jamestown. Then called "Allen's Brick House". it has been known, ever since this occupancy, as "Bacon's Castle".

There is a legend that says Arthur Allen, instead of being the English commoner that records indicated he was, actually might have been a Prince of the House of Hanover. Allegedly, he loved the same girl his twin brother loved, and when he found out that she favored his brother, he stabbed him, came to Virginia under an assumed name and started a new life, building his castle and raising a family.

Now operated by the Association for the Preservation of Virginia Antiquities, this imposing brick structure was built some time after 1655. It stands amidst a large grove of oaks. There are two expansive, paneled first floor rooms, two more rooms on the second floor, and what has been described as a "dungeon-like" attic on the third.

There are several interesting love stories associated with Bacon's Castle — ranging from romantic to bitter sweet to tragic. Consider, for example, the relationship of Emmet (or Emmitt) Robinson and his wife Indigo (Indy). There is a window at the castle inscribed with a poem Dr. Robinson etched to his wife: "In storm or sunshine — joy and strife, thou art my own, my much loved wife, treasure blessings of my life."

There is the Civil War romance of Virginia Hankins, whose father owned the house at the time, and the dashing young Confederate soldier, Sidney Lanier, who later was to become one of the South's most famous and most eloquent poets.

Stationed nearby, Lanier was a frequent visitor in 1863 and 1864, and became entranced with the lovely and well educated "Ginna". He wrote to friends that they had become "soul-friends", and that, as he read the works of great poets to her, "she is in a perfect blaze of enthusiasm."

Often during this idyllic interlude from the horrible war being waged around them, Ginna and Sidney would ride off into the green woods of Surry County, picnic, talk and plan. Lanier affectionately called her his "Little Brown Bird". And when, in August 1864, he was called away with his unit he pledged to return as soon as possible so they could be married.

They wrote to each other frequently but when Mrs. Hankins died, Ginna felt her first responsibility was to care for her grief-stricken father and his seven young sons. Sadly, she rejected Lanier's proposal. Still, although he eventually married, and created the works which are revered to this day, they corresponded faithfully for the rest of their lives in the form of poetry.

The third love story, though unsubstantiated, nevertheless has been passed down for generations. During the 1800s, a young girl was forced to meet her sweetheart, a boy from a nearby farm, in secret on the other side of a cornfield, because her father did not approve of him. Despite the predicament, Bacon's Castle hostesses will tell you, they shared the joy of young love and some measure of happiness.

That is, until one ill-fated evening when the girl was returning to the castle later than usual and had to light a candle to ascend the stairs leading to her room. She tripped on the stairs, and her long hair caught fire from the candle's flame. She didn't scream for help for fear of incurring the wrath of her father. Instead, she fled from the house in a state of shock, and ran through the cornfield desperately trying to reach her sweetheart. But by the time she got there she had been burned critically, and she died in his arms.

Is it any wonder, then, that in a setting of so much tragedy, anguish and lost love, there are so many occurrences of psychic phenomena?

Accounts of hauntings at the castle have been passed along, generation to generation, for more than 300 years. Many of those who have experienced strange sightings, noises, and "presences", believe they are manifestations of the devil. Others have felt it may be the spectral returning of Bacon's men, still seeking redress of the grievances they held against Governor Berkeley and the Colony so many years ago. Whatever, it is undisputed fact that the happenings which have occurred at the castle through the centuries have taken many forms.

Consider the revelations of Mrs. Charles Walker Warren, whose family once owned the castle. When she was a young woman, early in the 20th century, a visiting Baptist preacher who was spending the night, stayed up late reading his Bible. Sometime in the wee hours of the morning he heard footsteps descending the stairs from the second floor. Someone or something, he said later, opened the parlor door and walked past him. He saw no one, but felt the strong sensation that he was not alone. Then, mysteriously, a red velvet-covered rocking chair began moving back and forward as if someone were sitting in it, though the preacher could see no one. He put down his Bible and shouted "get thee behind me Satan," and the rocking stopped immediately.

Mrs. Warren and a number of guests reported hearing footsteps on the stairs late at night many times. One guest distinctly heard "horrible moaning" in the attic directly above her bedroom, though she was assured the next morning that no one could have been in the attic.

On another occasion, Mrs. Warren came into the downstairs parlor one morning and found the glass globe from a favorite nickel-plated reading lamp had been shattered into tiny fragments, yet, strangely, not a drop of kerosene from it had spilled onto the carpet. Also, a leather-bound dictionary had been "flung" across the room onto a sofa, and the iron stand upon which it normally rested had been hurled to a distant corner. No rational explanation could be offered to clear this up.

Richard Rennolds, curator of the castle from 1973 to 1981, used to tell of the time one morning at 3:30 when he was awakened by the sound of his two-and-a-half year old son laughing in his crib in an upstairs bedroom. "Daddy, where's the lady?" the child asked Rennolds when he reached him. "What lady?" Rennolds said. "The lady with the white hands. She was tickling me."

On another occasion, a few years later, a tour guide was standing in the great hall one morning before the castle was opened to the public when "something" ran by her from the outside passageway and went through the hall and into another

Illustration by Isabel Pettingill

118

chamber on the other side. She heard feet running on the hardwood floor but did not see anyone. As the sound of the steps were passing by, something brushed her arm and gave her a chill.

The same hostess also said there had been strange noises a number of times, most commonly loud popping and crackling sounds, which sometimes were heard by people in the video reception room. They were too much for one young couple who heard the noise and became so frightened they left the castle even before the tour started.

These and several other incidents, however, serve merely as preambles to the most shocking supernatural appearance at Bacon's Castle; one that reappears regularly at varying intervals over the years and has been seen and documented by a number of credible witnesses from several different generations.

It takes the form, say those who have seen it and been terrified by it, of a "pulsating, red ball of fire". It apparently rises near or from the graveyard of Old Lawne's Creek Church a few hundred yards south of the castle, soars about 30 to 40 feet in the air — always on dark nights — and then moves slowly northward. It seems to "float or hover" above the castle grounds before slowly moving back toward the ivy-covered walls of the ruins of Lawne's Creek Church, where it disappears.

One eyewitness, G. I. Price, a former caretaker at the castle, described the phenomenon to a local newspaper reporter in this manner: "I was standing, waiting in the evening for my wife to shut up the chickens, when a light about the size of a jack-me-lantern came out of the old loft door and went up a little . . . and traveled by, just floating along about 40 feet in the air toward the direction of the old graveyard."

Skeptics, of course, contend that the fireball is merely some form of physical manifestation that can be explained scientifically. But those who have seen it, including members of the Warren family and others, could never be convinced that it was not of a mystical, spiritual nature. Some even called it an appearance of the "Prince of Darkness".

One guest reportedly had "the wits frightened out of him" one night when the fiery red ball sailed into his bedroom at the castle, circled over his bed several times and then disappeared out the open window. A former owner of the castle told of seeing the fireball blaze overhead and enter his barn. Fearful of it igniting his stored hay, he ran toward the barn. Then the bright, glowing light turned and headed back toward the graveyard. In the 1930s, members of a local Baptist church, meeting at an evening revival session, collectively saw the strange sphere. It is said the praying that night was more intense than ever before in the congregation's memory.

What is the origin of this eerie fireball and why does it reappear every so often? One legend has it that a servant a century or so ago was late with his chores and as he was walking home in the darkness the red object overcame him, burst, and "covered him with a hellish mass of flames," burning him to death.

Another theory is that the light was somehow tied to hidden money in the castle. Some money was found years ago when two men were removing some bricks from the fireplace hearth in the second floor's west room. Apparently only a few people ever saw, or knew about the money, and since it was found, no one has seen the light. Still others say it may be associated with the spirit of Ginna Hankins going to the church where she and her sweetheart, Sidney Lanier, often lingered. Or could it be a recreation of the flaming hair of the young girl who ran to her lover across the cornfields so long ago?

Many oldtimers, however prefer to believe that the fireball is a periodic reminder of the brilliant comet that flashed across the same skies more than 300 years ago, forewarning that tragedy and bloodshed would soon follow. There are, in fact, those who are convinced that spirits frequent Bacon's Castle to this day; sad spirits from long ago, still seeking relief from their troubled and grief-stricken past.

The Legends of Great Dismal Swamp

Whoever named the Great Dismal Swamp knew exactly what they were doing. For the past three and a half centuries or so, it has been described by those who have been there, both the famous and the infamous, in the darkest, most brooding terms. Colonel William Byrd II, dispatched there to help designate the line dividing Virginia and North Carolina, wrote: "It is a horrible desert, with foul damps ascending without ceasing, corrupting the air, and rendering it unfit for respiration . . . having vapours which infest the air and causing ague and other distempers to the neighboring inhabitants. Toward the center of it no beast or bird approaches, nor so much as an insect or reptile exists. Not even a turkey buzzard will venture to fly over it, no more than the Italian vultures will over the filthy Lake Avernus, or the birds of the Holy Land over the salt sea, for fear of noisesome exhalations that rise from the vast body of nastiness."

Authors have painted the Great Dismal Swamp as alluring, capricious and contradictory. One wrote of the swamp that, "Like a beautiful woman, she tantalizes with her oft changing moods. She encourages recklessness, but metes out swift and cruel punishment to those whom she lures into her web of dangers. . . . She sadistically sears their souls with wounds which never heal. Wounds which forever must be soothed through distorted imaginations, tall tales, and uncontrolled enthusiasm for anything pertaining to the swamp."

Another writer years ago said Great Dismal was "an almost impenetrable wilderness, a treacherous bog, refuge of deadly snakes and every kind of wildlife. Here fled the wanted men and runaway slaves and those who would abandon the company of man. Many were never heard of again for the grim wilderness seldom gave of its secrets."

Harriet Beecher Stowe, who wrote "Uncle Tom's Cabin", also penned a novel about a slave crouching in Dismal Swamp.

Professional slave catchers in Norfolk brought their hounds to run down such hapless creatures, and the yelling and baying of the bloodhounds added to their terror.

The jungle-like undergrowth in some places is so dense, says another writer, "that man may become hopelessly lost a short distance from trails, canals, or roads. There is still real danger from poisonous snakes and wild animals. Some places are dangerous because of beds of quicksand. There are at times many dangerous cauldrons of smouldering peat. Each year some hunters or careless sightseers become lost, and often lose their lives."

There are indeed common tales of huge Eastern black bears attacking human victims, cracking their skulls with a single swipe from their massive paws. Many people firmly believe that there are bats in the quagmire which suck people's blood. In Colonial days, Great Dismal was said to be teeming with wild life. As one journalist put it, "Its tangled Juniper and canebrake were hung with snakes, and serpents fell without a warning hiss out of trees onto boats."

Despite all these sinister descriptions, however, the swamp also has a haunting beauty about it. It has been called a geological wonder, and a well balanced small world of strange, mystic charm, "teeming with reptiles, large and small animals, beautiful birds, delicate aromatic wildflowers, giant trees, and beautiful ferns."

It once was the home of majestic stands of juniper and cypress trees, but most of these have been cut down for timber. Today, Great Dismal is a 120,000-acre reserve, about 40 miles long and 15 miles wide, on the Virginia, North Carolina line which borders Suffolk and Chesapeake along its northern limits. At its heart is huge Lake Drummond, named for a Colonial governor of North Carolina who discovered it while hunting, and later was summarily hanged by Governor Berkeley of Virginia.

Great Dismal is not a swamp in the conventional sense, in that instead of having streams of water running into it, seven good sized rivers flow outward, and a large portion of the land is dry and as much as 20 feet above sea level. Although man has made severe environmental encroachments on the swamp, including many efforts to drain it, one led by George Washington, Great Dismal has endured. True, its once-great cypress and juniper trees have been lost to timber concerns, and the swamp's overall size has shrunk to less than half of what it was in the 1600s. Nevertheless, much of the land today remains unexplored and undisturbed.

More importantly, at least for the purposes of this book, is the fact that the rich, colorful legends of the swamp, passed down for more than 300 years, also have not only endured, but have thrived. And there are legions of these legends. Many originated with the Indians who once roamed here. Some told of "firebirds" abducting Indian maidens and great battles by famous warriors to overcome these supernatural beings. Other stories undoubtedly were spawned by the many slaves and fugitives from justice who sought refuge in the swamp, and by the hermits, recluses and eccentrics who have lived deep in the forest interiors. The countless thousands of hunters who have come to the swamp each season have unquestionably embellished such tales and added their own as they cooked dinner around their campfires on dark nights.

Numerous books, magazine pieces and newspaper articles have been written about such legends. The swamp is supposedly inhabited by spirits, witches, dragons, ghouls and ghosts. There are weird sights of bizarre and mysterious lights in the dense jungles and around Lake Drummmond, and all sorts of eerie

Photo courtesy U.S. Fish and Wildlife Service

123

sounds are heard at night time throughout the swamp.

Skeptics say the combination of alcohol, vivid imaginations, and such natural phenomena as methane gas, fireflies, and the glowing eyes and sounds of wild animals likely account for the great majority of strange sights and noises. But many steadfastly swear there are other, inexplicable causes for what they have seen and heard and no amount of scientific explanations will ever convince them otherwise.

Herewith, then, is a sampling of some of the better known tales of the swamp, which have survived the test of time.

* * * * *

The Fishing Bride

aptain Bill Crockett, a one-time merchant mariner who settled in the Great Dismal Swamp after World War I, first as a lumberman and later as a hunting guide, often told the story of a beautiful maiden who lived at the edge of the swamp near Washington's Ditch. On the morning of her wedding day, her fiance, a fearless lumberjack, set off into the forest to kill a deer for the reception feast.

When the prospective groom didn't return at the wedding hour, the maiden assured the guests he would be back, and as they continued partying, she slipped off into the swamp, in her wedding gown, to search for him. Neither was ever seen again. Over the intervening years, numerous hunters and others have claimed to see a mysterious apparition on the south side of Lake Drummond. In the early morning, as the first pale shafts of light dart through the trees, a transparent beautiful maiden, resplendent in white wedding gown, appears in the misty dawn and "glides" out onto a log several feet into the water, where she calmly baits her hook, casts her line out and patiently waits, to catch a fresh fish for her lover's breakfast.

* * * * *

The Untimely Death of Black Jack - the Hermit

Snow blanketed the swamp one Christmas Eve shortly after the turn of the 20th century, cloaking the trees and vines in a pure white shroud. Late in the afternoon, a hermit who lived at the edge of the forest and who was known only as "Black Jack", set out in his small boat with his faithful hunting dog, rowed across Lake Drummond and then went down Washington Ditch a few miles. Near White Marsh Road, they landed and walked into the thick woods in search of a deer for dinner.

Then a strange thing happened. The dog flushed the largest white buck Jack had ever seen. White deer are legendary in the swamp. Indians say they are protected by "the spirits". Perhaps so, because the buck froze in its tracks within a few feet of Jack and he fired at near point blank range, the bullet piercing the deer's chest. Instead of falling, however, the deer didn't even flinch. It turned and romped freely into the woods, and the dog immediately lost its trail. Jack was shaken.

Sometime later the dog chased a huge red buck and this time the hunter's shot rang true. By the time he got the deer into the boat and started home, it was almost dark. As he approached the center of the lake, a bluish-green halo of light appeared in the sky just above the tree tops. It first seemed to be the moon rising, but then the light moved rapidly toward the boat and hovered directly overhead, illuminating the whole lake like a giant spotlight. The grizzled old hermit was frightened, and he rowed quickly to shore.

He carried the heavy buck to his cabin, dropped it outside the door and ordered his dog to stand watch while he prepared to clean and dress it. Inside, he started a fire, got out of his cold wet clothes and sharpened his knives. When he opened the door both his dog and the deer were gone. Odd, because the dog would have barked at any disturbance. He got his lantern and began a search for the missing animals. He found small patches of blood in a snow trail that led back to the lake's edge where he had tied his boat. It appeared that the deer and the dog had entered the lake. Again, Jack was stunned.

As he stood there trying to figure things out, he heard a low moan. It grew louder and seemed to be coming from the center of Lake Drummond. As he looked out, the eerie bluish-green halo of light seemed to rise out of the water and soar gracefully through the air to a spot just above a giant cypress. It increased in brightness and lighted the tree with its glow.

Jack stood entranced by the spectacle. His hypnotic state was finally broken by the blood curdling scream of a wildcat. Shivering in the cold, Jack jumped in his boat, rowed across the lake, entered the feeder ditch and raced downstream to the locks. He tied up his boat and took the trail down the south side of the canal at Arbuckle's Landing, where he ran to Captain Crockett's cottage. He arrived at midnight, so cold and frightened he wasn't able to talk for three hours. Finally, after being warmed by the fire and a liquid mixture of honey, swamp water and moonshine, he blurted out the story of what had happened.

Jack left the next morning in search of his lost dog and the missing deer. That night, Captain Crockett dreamed of the mysterious white deer and the halo of light. It came to him as a premonition that Jack was in danger, so the next morning he went to check on his friend. At the hermit's cabin, he found the door open and the fire out. He then hurried to the edge of the lake where Jack kept his boat. There, he saw some tracks. he traced them into the thicket and there he found Jack, in a kneeling position, frozen to death. There were no signs of a struggle and no other tracks.

Captain Crockett said that since that time, on Christmas Eves between midnight and two in the morning, Jack can be heard gibbering about the white deer and the halo of light. And, at the break of dawn on Christmas mornings, the young red buck and Jack's dog can be seen near where his body was found. Crockett's story allegedly has been verified by many area hunters who claim they have fired at the deer but have never hit him. The dog and the buck vanish in the underbrush.

* * * * *

The Ghosts Who Speak French

here are several accounts about the ill-
fated French treasure ship, one of which
was published in the South Atlantic Quarterly some years ago.

Blown off course during a voyage in the 17th century, and chased by a British warship, the French vessel sought refuge in the Chesapeake Bay, and then was followed up the Elizabeth River, where it ran aground in the mouth of Deep Creek.

Laden with a plundered cargo of Dutch and Spanish gold coins, the French sailors abandoned ship, hauling as much treasure as they could carry, and headed into the Dismal Swamp. They buried their loot near the entrance, a theory strengthened by the fact that several caches of coins have been recovered there over the past 300 years. But soon after this had been done, the pursuing English seamen caught up with them and killed them.

Since them, even to the present day, many swamp natives, hunters, and visitors have reported hearing echoes of voices speaking in French near the entrance. The voices have been described as "having no earthly habitation". The general belief is that they belong to the slain French sailors who have returned to the swamp to eternally guard the remainder of their gold.

* * * * *

The Fabled White Deer

By far the most popular and most often repeated legend of Great Dismal Swamp is that of the handsome Indian brave and the beautiful white deer who walk through the woods side by side. They have reportedly been seen by literally hundreds of witnesses over the years, but no one has ever gotten close to them. They are forever protected by rattlesnakes.

The tale, as recounted by the indefatigable Captain Crockett and many others, is one of tragic and eternal love. It goes like this: Each autumn, two warring Indian tribes would declare a truce long enough for their braves to bag enough wild game to last through the winter. Squaws were not permitted to enter the forest because the tribes believed this to be an evil omen.

Wa-Cheagles was the daughter of one of the great chiefs — Sheew-a-nee, and over the years she had developed an unusual relationship with an old doe affectionately known as Cin-Co, which meant guiding friend. It was Cin-Co, the Indians believed, who led the plentiful deer to the swamp every fall.

Cin-Co also would lead her new fawn to the Indian princess each year. They always met at the edge of the forest in a small opening near a pool of dark brown water.

But one year as Wa-Cheagles waited for the annual rendez-vous, Cin-Co showed up alone and she was limping. The graceful and tame red deer touched the princess with her wet nose and then ran back toward the edge of the thicket. She did this two or three times. She wanted Wa-Cheagles to follow her, but the princess was apprehensive because by tradition she knew she wasn't supposed to go.

Still, she feared some harm had come to Cin-Co's fawn, and so, at last, she went with the deer deep into the woods. Finally, they came to a little clearing and Cin-Co stopped. There, Wa-Cheagles saw the little fawn standing with one foot on the head of a writhing, but barely alive rattlesnake. She surmised that Cin-Co had been bitten by the rattler, hence her limp, and that the deer wanted her to care for the fawn.

Then she heard a moan in the brush and saw an Indian warrior lying there with a swollen leg. He was a member of the hostile tribe and he, too, had been bitten. This created a dilemma. According to tribal custom, if Wa-Cheagles helped the fallen warrior she must pledge herself to him. And if she did this, they would be hunted down and shot with arrows tipped with the venom of a water moccasin.

Despite the obvious dangers, she removed her beret and tied it tightly around the brave's leg. She then found some snakeroot and applied a crude poultice to cover the wound. Then, as she turned to rejoin her tribe, she noticed that the fawn had disappeared and that Cin-Co had died. Crying, she made her way back to camp.

For the next three days, Wa-Cheagles slipped away to tend the wounded brave. But on the third day her father appeared in the clearing. They embraced, and the father left, carrying off the carcass of Cin-Co. Wa-Cheagles knew he would be helpless to save her, but that he was giving the couple time to escape.

So she and her new mate made their way to the edge of Lake Drummond where they rested. But soon they were confronted by three braves from Wa-Cheagles' tribe. They had been sent to remove the curse from their tribe. Wa-Cheagles and the warrior faced them bravely, willing to accept their fate.

As the braves drew back their bows to complete their mission, a strange thing happened. Suddenly a dark cloud blotted out the sun and a loud rustling noise filled the air. An immense flock of wild geese swirled around the Indian maiden and her lover. Then the geese settled on the lake in a mass so thick no water could be seen. As the three braves dropped their bows and arrows and ran, terrified, into the forest, the "swamp spirit" arose from the lake and strode across the backs of the geese to approach Wa-Cheagles and the warrior.

The swamp spirit told them that the spirit of Cin-Co had saved them. Now, Wa-Cheagles must continue the good work of Cin-Co, so she would be transformed into a white deer, and would have a small crimson spot on her forehead, while her lover would become a "charmed hunter". Together, they would roam the swamp's forests forever, and would always be protected against animals and hunters.

It is thus the spiritual apparitions of the white doe and her brave lover who have often been sighted as they walked through the tangled jungles of the swamp together. Many hunters have sighted them and a number have tried to follow them, but they always disappear, as if by magic. The hunters who have pursued them, however, to a man, swear they have always encountered a rattlesnake at the spot where they sighted them!

* * * * *

The White Canoe

nd, finally, there is the ever-lasting romantic legend of the Indian brave and his maid who were reunited after her death, and who often have been seen in their pristine white canoe at midnight on the waters of Lake Drummond. This tale was immortalized by the famous Irish poet, Sir Thomas Moore, who spent some time at the swamp in the early 1800s, and penned the following — "A Ballad - The Lake of the Dismal Swamp".

They made her a grave too cold and damp,
  For a soul so warm and true;
She has gone to the Lake of the Dismal Swamp,
Where all night long, by the fire-fly lamp,
  She paddles her white canoe.
Her fire-fly lamp I soon shall see,
  Her paddle I soon shall hear;
Long, Long, and loving our lives shall be,
I'll hide the maid in a cypress-tree,
  When the footstep of Death is near.
Away to the Dismal Swamp he speeds;
  His path was rugged and sore,
Through tangled juniper, beds of reeds,
And many a fen where the serpent feeds,
  And man never trod before.
And when on the ground he sunk to sleep —
  If slumber his eyelids knew —
He lay where the deadly vine doth weep
Its venomous tear, and nightly steep
  The flesh with blistering dew.
And near him the she-wolf stirred the brake,
  The coppersnake breathed in his ear;
Till starting, he cries, from his dreams awake,
'Oh! when shall I see the dusky lake,
  And the white canoe of my dear?
He saw the lake, and a meteor bright
  Quick over its surface played;
'Oh, welcome,' he cried, 'my dear one's light!'
And the dim shores echoed for many a night
  The name of the death-cold maid.
He hollowed a boat of the birchen bark,
  Which carried him off from the shore;
Far, far, he followed the meteor spark,
The winds were high and the clouds were dark,
  And the boat returned no more.
But oft from the Indian hunter's camp
  This maid and her lover so true,
Are seen, at the hour of midnight damp,
To cross the lake by a fire-fly lamp,
  And paddle their white canoe.

Uplifting Spirits at the Shipyard

t is rare when someone suffers physical harm from a ghost. Experts believe the great majority of spirits — as many as 98 percent of them — are basically friendly. Once in a great while a story will surface about a maddened poltergeist, or noisy ghost, who, in venting his or her wrath over a past slight or grievance, will slap, hit, claw or choke someone. The notorious Bell Witch of Tennessee comes to mind.

More often if someone does get injured in a psychical occurrence it is by accident. When objects start flying around, either thrown by poltergeists, or caused by the phenomenon called psycho-kinesis, in which human beings have the power to move things without physical contact, there is always the danger of getting hit by anything from a wet dish towel to a marble topped table.

But in the case of the alleged ghost who stalks the Norfolk Naval Shipyard, there was an instance where a person had to be hospitalized due to his own fear. It is said to have happened sometime before World War I when a sailor, leaving the duty office on the second floor of building number 33 saw an apparition moving down the hallway toward a wide, dark staircase that had been carved out of deck planks from a 19th century ship. The unfortunate sailor was so scared he fell down the stairs and broke his leg!

He was one of scores of military and civilian employees at the shipyard who have either sensed the presence of, or glimpsed the transparent image of a ghost known as "John Paul". The specter was named for the great American naval hero of Revolutionary War fame, John Paul Jones, because he appeared, to those who claim to have seen him, in military dress of that era — black boots, knickers, a long blue tunic and a dark-colored Napoleonic hat.

Many people have sighted his "fleeting image" or sensed that "someone was watching them" in buildings 29, 31, and

33. All of those who have had such an experience ask not to be identified; a fact that has frustrated public affairs officer Joe Law, who has tried to track down the legends for a history of the shipyard he is writing.

"I'm convinced there is absolutely no doubt in their minds that they have witnessed something out of the ordinary," Law says, "but they don't want to be quoted." A woman administrator who had worked at the yard for three decades, for example, said that once, in the 1960s, she felt the presence "most distinctly". She had been filing drawings in building 31, when, suddenly, "I felt like someone was watching me, and when I turned around, I saw a shadow," she said. It was a man's shadow although the features were undistinguishable.

Years later a young lady who worked for the administrator had the same sensation, only she saw the apparition more clearly, later describing it in explicit detail. It fit the classic description of John Paul. "We decided it was the old boy coming back to check that we were doing the shipyard work right,"

said the administrator.

While John Paul is the one who has been most often sighted, there are, apparently, other spirits which occasionally roam the shipyard. One has been seen on the waterfront, where the nation's first drydock was constructed in 1767. Some attribute "his" origin to the finding, years ago, of three intact coffins containing the remains of British soldiers which were unearthed during 1971 excavations near drydocks 1 and 2. It is speculated that the soldiers had died on an English ship and were buried there sometime in the 18th century. Shipyard workers say their caskets were reburied in a cemetery at the Naval Hospital.

Naval spokesman Law says there are other reasons for the possible appearances of spirits. He says some of the original land may have included Indian burial grounds, and that there were likely many transient grave sites in the marsh lands near the waterfront. The government also took over several old farm houses and there possibly were family cemeteries in the area.

Other workers at the shipyard say the ghost of an old soldier, believed to have died in a jail at the site, possibly of Civil War vintage, has returned on occasion. One veteran employee believes he comes back to keep watch in one of two towers atop the barracks. "He sometimes sits in the little tower up there," the worker said.

Law says he once interviewed a woman who experienced strange manifestations in one of the homes, built in the 1830s, across the yard. Allegedly, in Quarters B, keys have moved on their own, windows have opened and shut, bolted doors have slammed, lights have flicked on and off, and other appliances have acted queerly. According to the woman, the spirits were disturbed each time a ring of large brass keys was not hung properly near the front door locks. Whenever the keys were left elsewhere, they mysteriously found their way back to the door. Whatever it was that caused this, it was enough, she added, to terrify the family dog.

And, finally, there are the "religious related" phenomena which occurred in an old sail loft, where, in another era, sailmakers practiced their craft. "We've heard noises like people driving grommets, and sewing machines turning on by themselves," cites one veteran employee. Muffled voices carry on ghostly conversations. "Everybody who is up here has heard it at night," the worker added.

One old time sailmaker even saw a "cloud" which filled the entire loft. He said it lasted a week, was not caused by the weather outside, and resembled "the thick white steam of a locomotive". He claimed it was of spiritual origin, and likened it to the "shekinah", of the glory of God as scriptured in the Old Testament. The Bible said that when Moses led his people from Egypt to Canaan, God cloaked them in clouds during the day and fires at night to protect them from Pharaoh's armies.

And if people disbelieved that, the sailmaker said, what happened a year later should have convinced them. A fire erupted in the loft, sending flames several feet high. However, it only lasted a few minutes, and when it was put out, nothing was destroyed! This sign was certainly enough for the sailmaker. "Everybody else was mystified," he noted. "I was given peace. You would call it uplifting."

A Case of
Crisis Apparition

t is a shaded, secluded "isle of serenity" amidst the hustle and bustle of downtown Norfolk. It has been that way for 350 years. In fact, the first church built on the site of the present-day St. Paul's was known as "Ye Chappell of Ease". It was erected in 1641 as part of the Elizabeth River Parish. Norfolk became a borough in 1736, and the present church, known as the Borough Church, was built in 1739.

The church was struck and partially burned by the British on January 1, 1776, when Norfolk was bombarded and destroyed. The building was serving as a shelter for women and children during the attack. In the Civil War, Federal forces occupied the church from 1862 to 1865. The one and three-quarter acre church yard is very similar to the old yards of England. There are 274 listed graves here, the oldest of which is that of Dorothy Farrell, who died on January 18, 1673. Some of the stone markers bear a skull and crossbones, which signified death, not the resting place of a pirate.

Wedged into the far northeast corner of the church yard is an above ground tombstone with a strange quotation carved into it.

"Yes," says a church spokesman when asked, "that was a tragic case. The poor man lost his whole family. It is our only ghost story."

It also was, apparently, a case of "crisis apparition." This occurs when a person — the "receiver" — suddenly becomes aware that another person — the "transmitter" — is undergoing a crisis. This may be in the form of pain, shock, emotion or death, even though the transmitter may be some distance away; in some cases thousands of miles. The most common examples of such phenomena occur in times of war, when a mother, for example, may report seeing or hearing her son at the moment he is wounded, often at the instant of his death. The theory is that the pain and shock trigger off involuntary telepathic contact between son and mother, or transmitter and receiver.

David Duncan's crisis apparition occurred in 1823. Three years earlier he had married Martha Shirley, the daughter of a widow who operated the Norfolk boarding house where he often stayed. Duncan was captain of the cargo schooner Sea Witch, and he took his bride on a honeymoon voyage to several Mediterranean ports. Afterwards, they settled in Norfolk and she gave birth to twins, Davis and Ann. Early in 1823, Duncan set sail again on a merchant voyage, carrying a cargo of lumber and animal hides.

On the night of May 12th, the Sea Witch was anchored in the harbor of Genoa, Italy. Most of the crew had gone ashore to unwind, but master Duncan had stayed behind, reading in his cabin from the 18th century poet Edward Young's "Night Thoughts on Life, Death and Immortality". It was eerily apropos.

Thousands of miles away, a fire broke out in the bakery beneath the Duncan's rooms. Martha desperately tried to escape with her infants, but a rickety staircase collapsed, and they perished in the flames. At that precise instant David Duncan was reading the poet's lines describing Death as an "insatiate archer" when he envisioned a fire at the foot of the main

H I
Mrs M.A.E. DUNCAN
wife of D Duncan
Ob 12th May 1823 Æt 19
also her two infant children
Insatiate archer! could not one suffice?
Thy shaft flew thrice and thrice my peace was slain

mast. He ran from his cabin and when he reached the deck the fire seemed to blossom. In the midst of the flames he clearly saw the wraith-like form of his wife frantically clutching their son and daughter.

Her screams pierced the silence in the harbor. "David! David! Save us!" she cried. And then, in a flash she was gone, as was the fire. Although crazed with anxiety, it was not until sometime later, when his ship finally docked at Norfolk, that Duncan learned the awful horror of his illusion was real.

And so, he placed a horizontal, raised tombstone, inscribed with Martha's name and the date of death over the single grave site in St. Paul's church yard. To this, he had the stone-maker carve the two lines of verse he had been reading when his loved ones died: "Insatiate archer, could not one suffice? Thy shaft flew thrice and thrice my peace was slain."

CHAPTER 24

The Mad Poltergeist of Portsmouth

t was known simply as the house on Florida Street in the Mount Hermon section of Portsmouth.

It was torn down several years ago.

It probably is just as well.

There was a time, nearly 30 years ago when the old house at 949 Florida Avenue was the talk not only of the town, but of the entire country. For a brief period, in September 1962, the residence became a whirlwind of psychic activity which lasted several days, frightened the wits out of the chief of police and newspaper reporters, among others, and drew unruly crowds of hundreds who demanded to see what was going on.

It had begun, simply enough, on a Thursday afternoon about 4 p.m. Charles and Annie Daughtery were living in the house at the time with their great-great-grandson. The Daughterys were described as being very old; Annie was said to be close to 100. A little horse vase, sitting on a sewing machine in the hallway, fell on the floor three or four times. Annie, who said she didn't know what ghosts or haunted houses were, and was not afraid of them, told her great-great-grandson to take the vase and set it outside. Just then a bottle of hair lotion inexplicably sailed through the air and struck her in the back of the head.

By the next day accounts of the mysterious happenings had circulated through the neighborhood and beyond, and came to the attention of local newspaper reporters. It had been alleged that: a carpet eerily rose off the floor by itself; vases jumped from mantlepieces and hurtled over people's heads; and a mattress slid off a bed and onto the floor, all in front of the incredulous Annie Daughtery. But the phenomena had not been witnessed by her alone. Friends and neighbors had seen these occurrences, too, although many didn't stay long. They had fled in stark fear. One who reportedly had run out of the house was the local chief of police!

By Saturday the events had become so celebrated that when Joseph Phillips, a Virginian-Pilot staff writer, entered the house along with a photographer, a mob of more than 200 people had gathered outside. "I didn't believe in ghosts — until Saturday," Phillips began his front page article. But, he added, he "got goose pimples while dodging flying household objects that crashed to bits on the floor. I saw weird things happen, but I don't know what caused them."

When Phillips entered the house, he stood by a buffet with Mrs. Marion Bivens, a neighbor. She asked him if he had felt the buffet move. She looked scared. He hadn't felt anything. Suddenly a vase that had been on the mantlepiece in the living room crashed into the hallway wall at the front of the house, apparently rounding a corner in the process. Phillips and the photographer ran to the living room. There was no one there. As they did, a cup from the buffet in the dining room shattered at their feet. At this point, Mrs. Bivens ran from the house in terror.

"Then I saw an empty tobacco can fly toward me from the buffet," Phillips said. "It was in the air when I saw it. It crashed and rolled to the floor at my feet."

Phillips' subsequent story of his experience drew even more people to the area, and when a wire services article ran a day or two later, crowds grew to enormous proportions. Police estimated 20,000 people congregated there one day, and they ordered out the fire department, hoses ready, in case a riot broke out. Some in the horde of people stormed inside the house and demanded to "see the thing." A number were arrested, and finally the Daughterys had to move out of the house themselves and stay with relatives until the excitement died down.

William G. Roll, a scientist with the Parapsychology Lab at Duke University, showed up to investigate. He said there were enough witnesses to support the likelihood that the disturbances in the house were caused by Recurrent Spontaneous Psycho-kinesis, or RSPK. But Roll claimed the flying objects and loud noises were not necessarily the work of a ghost. Rather, he believed they were the work of the living not the dead.

"Our focus on RSPK eruptions has been on the individual

who is at the center of the disturbances," he told a reporter, adding that usually such occurrences are sparked by tension or certain neurological features.

Maybe so, but that would have been a difficult theory to swallow by any of the dozens of people who were in the little house on Florida Avenue during the few days all hell broke loose. They didn't have a rational explanation, but they knew what they saw. As reporter Joseph Phillips summed it up, "I didn't believe this nonsense before. Now I'm not so sure."

An Omnibus of Olde Towne Haunts

Even if you have little or no interest in ghosts, a trip to the Olde Towne section of Portsmouth is well worth the time. It is a fascinating, well-preserved repository of some of the most elegant early-American architecture in the nation, with superb examples of Colonial, Federal, Greek Revival, Georgian and Victorian houses. Home owners obviously have taken great pride in their dwellings, yards and gardens in this one square mile antique oasis, and there is just enough wrought-iron flavor to remind one of New Orleans' famous French Quarter. It also is conveniently near the Olde Harbour Market, and Portsmouth's answer to Norfolk's Waterside — Portside, complete with food, libations and assorted entertainment.

Patents of land in the Olde Towne area were begun as early as 1659 by Captain William Carver, a master mariner, ship owner, and ardent patriot, who was later hanged for his part in Bacon's Rebellion. Because of Carver's indiscretions, his lands were forfeited to the crown, and, in 1716, a portion of them was granted to Colonel William Crawford (for whom Crawford Parkway was named). He was a prominent merchant and ship owner of the region, and in 1752 he set aside approximately 65 acres from his vast plantation and laid off the little town called Portsmouth. Because of its proximity to the Elizabeth River, the area now known as Olde Towne became the central site of the city's early development. And, as it states, accurately, in a local tourist brochure, ". . . a sense of Portsmouth's past still lingers in the warm, worn brick of the English basement homes and the aged elegance of the luxuriant magnolia trees. We invite you to explore this intriguing area and share in the wealth of history and fine architecture that it encompasses."

Now, if you are interested in ghosts — and that's presumably a "given" since you are reading this book — Olde Towne is a veritable gold mine with perhaps the greatest concentration of supernatural spirits in the country, if not the world! At last count there were something like 27 separate specters haunting the houses within this few-square-block area. And little wonder. What a marvelous setting they have, amidst all the gargoyles and turrets, the dank basements and musty attics.

The rich, colorful tales of their deeds have been told and retold through generations of families here, and resulted, a few years ago, in the creation of an annual Ghost Walk which takes place each Halloween. Local residents, and sometimes actors, recreate many of the more dramatic stories. The tour starts at the old Trinity Church yard at Court and High Streets, among the tombstones, after dark on the Friday closest to Halloween. A book entitled "Ghost Stories of Olde Towne Portsmouth, Virginia", has recently been published by the Civic League of Portsmouth. It is recommended reading. Herewith, then, is a sampler of the hauntings . . . .

*****

The Grieved Slave at Grice-Neely House

hosts seem to follow Cathi Bunn around in Olde Towne. When she and her family lived at the house at 418 Crawford Street, for instance, the sound of violin music often was heard wafting from the attic, although the mystery musician was never found. Cathi, a vivacious young woman who directed the annual Ghost Walks for a number of years, says a visiting aunt was awakened in the house one night and witnessed an "animated, but silent, conversation between two seafarers". There also was the recurring phenomenon of the chandelier. Its lights would frequently turn on and burn brightly by themselves, after having been turned off. Electricians could offer no plausible explanation.

Then, in 1987, the Bunns moved to the Grice-Neely house at 202 North Street. The first portion of this English basement home is said to have been built sometime between 1750 and 1760, and it still contains some original wooden-pegged rafters.

Curiously, a well-worn tombstone serves as a step in front of the house. It once marked the grave of an infant who was buried somewhere in the yard, although Cathi has never found the exact location. Grice-Neely has been restored to its previous splendor and evokes the atmosphere of New Orleans through the exquisite grill work of its wrought iron balcony and its graceful staircase.

Interestingly, there is a place on the rear facade of the building where a rather large window has been bricked over. Cathi says that in the 1850s a medium held a reading in the house and told the owners that when the next person living there died, they should be lowered out of this window and then it should be taken out and paved over with brick. By doing this, the family would forever ward off evil spirits. And apparently the family carried out the medium's direction to the letter.

Cathi became personally acquainted with the resident ghost of the house in a somewhat frightening manner. "I was all alone one night," she recalls, "and I decided to take a nice hot bath. I left the door slightly ajar, and I was enjoying myself, soaking, when I heard footsteps in the hallway outside. I said, 'Oh, no, there goes my peace and quiet. My husband and the kids are back.' But it wasn't them.

"The footsteps were distinct. It sounded like someone with no shoes on. It came right up to the bathroom door and then stopped. It threw a shadow across the doorway. Oh, man, I can tell you, I was scared. Then the steps continued, which was quite strange, because there was a solid wall where it kept walking! It took me a long time before I felt comfortable in the house alone again."

Her teenage daughter, Jennifer, also has experienced the "presence". One night she was doing her homework on her bed when it started to shake violently. She thought her younger brother was playing a trick on her, but she looked under the bed and around the room and there was no one there. "I got out of the room and didn't go back that night," she says.

Cathi adds that earlier tenants of the house also met the ghost — one of them face to face. "A college student was staying in what is now Jennifer's room," she says. "One night he woke up to find a black man standing at the foot of the bed with what the student called 'a puzzled look' on his face. Then he just dissolved, like a mist." A woman tenant once saw the same apparition standing on the circular staircase in the house. Then she realized she could see right through him!

There have been numerous other sightings. One resident was shaving, when he saw a black man standing behind him in the mirror's reflection. Again, the vision disappeared without a trace. Once a workman in the house saw a man peering into a living room window one cold February day. He didn't think much about it until later when he remembered the man wasn't wearing a shirt.

Cathi says one of her tenants was so frightened by the sounds of someone running across the attic floor above his room he wanted to keep a gun by his bed. "What's up there you can't shoot," she told him, "because I think it's already dead!"

In her efforts to track down the origins of the spirit, and why it is there, Cathi learned of a legend that clearly fits the description of what has been seen and heard in the house. It is, she believes, the ghost of a slave named Jemmy, who was stabbed to death in the early 1800s by his master, who was having an affair with Jemmy's wife.

He periodically reappears, Cathi believes, in search of his long lost love.

* * * * *

The Headless "Graduate"

W hat self-respecting ghost book would be complete without a headless horseman story?

By stretching one's imagination a little here and there, such a tale could be linked to the Ball-Nivison House in Olde Towne Portsmouth. The structure itself was built around 1780, and, according to a local tourist brochure, it is an ideal example of a "tax-dodger" house. That is, it has a gambrel roof; one with two slopes on each side, the lower slope steeper than the upper. The purpose was to make the house appear to have but a single story so as to avoid paying the heavy English taxes on a two-story edifice.

Bob Albertson's family has lived here for more than half a century, and for a long time during that period there was a resident ghost with very predictable habits. "We treated him just like another member of the family," Albertson says. "People can live with ghosts. They're not malevolent. He goes his way and I go mine.

"For a long time we never tried to pass it off as a haunted house. We consider ourselves reasonably normal people. But I have to admit, a number of things have happened in the house that aren't supposed to happen. I can't explain some of them," he adds. "We have never really been afraid. Let's

face it, I can be pretty frightening myself in the morning sometimes," Albertson says whimsically.

The manifestations he and others in his family have been subjected to over the years follow a precise pattern. His specter always goes one way — from library to the hall door. There, it lifts a heavy antique latch-lock adorned with a lion and unicorn, opens the door, walks up the steps and stops by Albertson's bedroom door. "I can tell you this," he says. "That latch is so heavy it couldn't blow open or open by itself.

"I can't explain it. It just happens. You are looking at over 200 years of inhabitants. There are a lot of lives that have passed through here." Oddly, he says, the psychic activity has slowed down considerably since the Albertsons opened up the house to the annual Olde Towne Ghost Walk held each Halloween. "It's been pretty quiet lately," he noted.

Such inactivity has not dampened the hopes of curiosity seekers who want to witness something supernatural first-hand. Many have stopped by the Ball-Nivison House and asked if they could come in and wait for something to happen. "Even if I tell them it has been several years since the last 'appearance', it doesn't seem to faze them," Albertson says. "They want to come in and look around anyway."

Where is the connection to the headless horseman? Only Albertson's mother has seen the phantasmal spirit, and she saw it only once. Appropriately enough, it was on an October night more than 20 years ago. It appeared to her wearing a black robe similar to a graduation gown, and it seemed to make the sound of labored breathing. This, says Albertson, was particularly strange, because the apparition was headless. A cap, "something like a mortar board", rested on its shoulders.

"For many years I have heard of a legend of a headless horseman riding down Glasgow Street in the dead of night," Albertson says. "Our house is almost at the foot of Glasgow, but I honestly don't know if there is any connection there. People make what they want of it."

* * * * *

Mike Hardy
Mends His Ways

One of the more colorful, yet least substantiated stories told during the annual Ghost Walk each Halloween in Olde Towne pertained to a local resident who fought for the Confederates in the Civil War. His name was Mike Hardy, and he was a swaggering braggart who often boasted about how many Yankees he had killed during the fighting. He did admit, however, that one of those who had died at his hands did occasionally gnaw at his conscience. It was a young drummer boy he had shot in the back.

After the war Hardy returned to Portsmouth and lived, as one reporter later phrased it, "a life full of carousing and lechery." Some years later, as the tale goes, the crusty ex-Reb was passing by St. Paul's Church when he suddenly felt a strong compulsion to ask forgiveness for his past sins. As he knelt in the unfamiliar position of prayer, he was startled to hear a voice behind him say, "I have long forgiven you for what you did to me."

Hardy turned and came face to face with the ghost of the drummer boy. The lad told him, "Change your ways Mike Hardy, or you won't be able to go where I am now!" Then he vanished. Appropriately awed by this omen, Hardy became an "upstanding citizen". And long after, as he lay dying on his bed, his doctor asked him why he had no fear of death. Hardy only smiled, because it is said he saw the Yankee drummer boy in the corner of the room, waiting to take him away.

* * * * *

A Prophesy of Death

Thy soul shall find itself alone

'Mid dark thoughts of the gray

tombstone

(Spirits of the Dead)

ow would you like to know the precise day on which you would die? That, apparently, is what happened to the Reverend John Braidfoot, a Scotsman who became the second rector of Trinity Church in Portsmouth in 1773. Following the Revolutionary War, during which he served as Chaplain of the Continental Army, Braidfoot had a difficult time maintaining his ministry. It was a time when many churches closed, but the Reverend continued to live in the rectory at the glebe and regularly visited his neighbors in need.

One night, while driving home in his buggy, his horse stopped suddenly. Blocking the road was what Braidfoot later described as an "apparition". There was an eerie silence, and then, in a rare occurrence, the apparition spoke. It told the Reverend that he would die at home on the following February 6th. The grim prophesy was repeated three or four times over the next few months.

According to the Reverend's great granddaughter, who recounted the story 150 years later in Margaret DuPont Lee's

marvelous book, "Virginia Ghosts", Mrs. Braidfoot decided to throw a dinner party on February 6th, to take her husband's mind off of death. In the midst of the festivities, Braidfoot excused himself and went up to his room. When he did not return, members of the party went up to look for him. He was dead!

CHAPTER 26

A Dying Daughter's Noisy Visitor

he great Norfolk yellow fever epidemic of 1855 is responsible, at least indirectly, for two melancholy tales of hauntings — one in Portsmouth and one in Norfolk. Norfolk had seen outbreaks of the dread disease on several previous occasions, including 1795, 1802, 1821, and 1826, but nothing had prepared them for the pending "Death Storm".

It was on June 7, 1855, that the steamer Ben Franklin, enroute from St. Thomas in the Virgin Islands to New York, and, experiencing engine troubles, put into port at Hampton Roads. When it became known that yellow fever was raging throughout St. Thomas, the ship was put into quarantine. Two weeks later it was allowed to enter Page and Allen's Shipyard near the Gosport Navy Yard on the condition that the captain keep his vessel sealed tight. However, he violated his agreement, opened his hatches and pumped out his bilges, which were swarming with the larvae of the deadly Aedes aegypti mosquito.

Within three weeks a shipyard worker who had entered the pestilence-laden hold of the Ben Franklin, died of yellow fever, and panic erupted across Hampton Roads, because at that time many people, including some leading authorities, thought the disease was contagious. (Its cause was not discovered for another 50 years by a native of Tidewater, Dr. Walter Reed, who was born in Gloucester). When more cases broke out in a tenement row of buildings near the shipyard, city authorities built a fence around the complex in hopes of preventing the fever's spread, which, of course, was fruitless. Prevailing winds carried the mosquitoes across the Elizabeth River into Portsmouth, and then to other sections of Norfolk, sparing neither rich nor poor. As the outbreak began to reach epidemic proportions, terror seized the population. In the hot summer months of July and August, literally thousands of people chose to evacuate, cramming trains and steamers. But then came word that they were not wanted in some areas.

New York, Washington, Baltimore, Richmond, Suffolk, and Petersburg all declared quarantines on Norfolkians, and there was one report that a boatload of people was repulsed at bayonet point while attempting to land at Old Point Comfort. The Eastern Shore and Mathews humanely accepted the frantic refugees, and by August 14, 1855, it was estimated that fully half the population of Norfolk had left the city.

By the end of August, what was left of the town had become one great hospital. From 70 to 100 people were dying daily and coffins and rough boxes were described as being "piled up like cord wood as high as a man could reach." At one point the supply of coffins gave out and the bodies had to be interred in boxes, in one instance, four to a box. The corpses were tied up in the blankets in which they died and carried out to the potter's field in furniture wagons, carts or drays to be buried layer upon layer in pits.

August 14th was set aside as a day of humiliation and prayer, but the fever continued to spread. The district south of Main Street was almost entirely deserted, and only a handful of merchants conducted business, most of them from their homes. Aside from the steady stream of coffins being carted, the streets of Norfolk were mostly deserted. The siege lasted through September and into late October and only abated when the first frost came. As one author put it, "Norfolk lay suffering, stunned, still unable to grasp the full meaning of the fearful calamity. Every man, woman and child, almost without exception, had been stricken by the fell fever, and about 2,000 had been buried."

One of those 2,000 was a young girl named Cathy, daughter of a grizzled old sea captain. After she had become afflicted with the fever they had taken her to a makeshift Red Cross center at 218 Glasgow Street, a large, three and a half story 18th century building now known as the Gaffos House. There, in the sweltering heat of the attic, the captain had poured his heart out in prayer for the daughter his wife had given her own life for in childbirth.

When Cathy died, the captain put out to sea for long months at a time. When he returned to Portsmouth on his infrequent visits, he would always walk by the house on Glasgow Street, pause, and stare up at the attic windows. It is said tears would stream down his ruddy cheeks.

About 30 years ago, George and Mary Alice Gaffos moved into the historic house with their two daughters, Andrea and Sabrina. The Gaffos both were natives of Portsmouth and had long dreamed of owning the house despite its sad background.

The children heard it first. After only a few weeks in the house, Andrea in particular, would tell George and Mary Alice that she heard heavy footsteps at night ascending the stairs leading up to the attic. Then she would hear the attic door slam. She said it was like someone with boots on. At first, the Gaffos thought it was the girls' imaginations. After all, the house was more than 200 years old, and prone to creaking noises.

But in time the noisy intruder made himself known to all in the household. Several months later, in the dead of winter,

George and Mary Alice were downstairs working on a crossword puzzle in front of the fireplace, when, suddenly, the front door slammed so hard it frightened both of them. Seconds later they heard the loud thumping of what sounded like heavy boots climbing the stairs. The Gaffos listened intently as the very distinct steps continued up to the fourth floor and then the attic door slammed shut.

George got a flashlight, and then he and his wife, scared as they were, managed to open the attic door. They searched the room following the light's strong beam, and were relieved to find no one there. Says Mary Alice, "we both just collapsed in each other's arms."

A month later the manifestations recurred in a slightly different manner. George was upstairs working on the third floor, Andrea was asleep in her bedroom, and Mary Alice and Sabrina were downstairs. Hearing distinct footsteps pacing back and forth in the attic, George called down to his wife asking her what the girls were doing in the attic. When she told him where they were, his face whitened. He said someone was in the house. He told them to get out immediately, and if they heard a gunshot they were to call the police. After they left, George nervously, but carefully, searched every inch of the attic, and then the entire house, but again, he found nothing.

Some time after that Andrea heard the strange noises, only this time they came from downstairs. She was in the house alone and didn't know what to do. She finally decided to make a dash down the stairs for the front door. As she got to the first floor, she happened to glance in the living room. There, the Gaffos' Australian Shepherd dog, Shelley, seemed to have cornered someone or something, although Andrea couldn't see anything. Shelley was barking and growling like crazy. Then the dog ran into the kitchen and continued to snarl at the invisible intruder. This went on for some minutes before Andrea fled the house.

On another occasion, George's mother-in-law, Mrs. Newton, was staying with the girls while the Gaffos were gone on a business trip. She slept in their room with her little dog beside her on a pillow. Sometime in the middle of the night she was awakened by a loud thumping. Thinking it might be her dog, she reached over only to find the dog wasn't there. She had heard the stories of the resident "ghost", but she did not fear the supernatural, and was determined to find the cause. She turned on the lights and saw her bedroom slippers being tossed up into the air over and over again. She could only gasp. The eerie spectacle lasted only a few seconds, but Mrs. Newton had seen enough. She couldn't get back to sleep until after the sun came up.

George says the spectral visits occur infrequently. "We'll go for months and nothing happens. Then we'll hear the front door slam and the footsteps going up the stairs. Then we know he's back.

Could it be the salty old captain, returning from yet another voyage, to once again visit his fever-stricken daughter?

* * * * *

If there was a "good" side to the devastating yellow fever epidemic of 1855, it was in the heroic and humanitarian effort of a number of people, including doctors, nurses, and ministers, who risked their own lives in attempting to bring relief to the epidemic sufferers. Some came to Norfolk and Portsmouth from out of town. One such noble person was Dr. Richard Blow from Tower Hill in Sussex County.

His two sisters, Mrs. George Blacknall and Mrs. Nimrod Hunter, lived in a large Greek Revival double house on Bute Street. When he arrived to treat the sick, he found them packing. They were going to escape the deadly plight, hopefully, by fleeing to their father's plantation in Sussex. Dr. Blow, therefore, had no problem in getting them to allow him to use their house as a temporary hospital. He worked tirelessly in his efforts to save lives, only to contract the disease himself. He died in the back parlor barely a few weeks after he had arrived.

His sisters returned once the threat was over and lived in the house for the rest of their lives. Mrs. Blacknall's daughters then inherited the estate and rented it to a woman who ran a boarding house there for a number of years. After World War I, Mrs. Blacknall's daughters sold the house, and it was then that their long-time woman renter told them about her "mysterious" experiences.

She said that on September 20th of the first year she lived there, just before retiring for the evening, she had a strange sensation that she was not alone. She looked toward a doorway that connected the two parts of the house and saw the apparition of what one writer described as a "sad-faced, portly, middle-aged man dressed in black standing there fingering his gold watch chain." Frightened, she cried out and as she did, the vision faded before her eyes.

She then said the same apparition appeared every year on the same date. The two daughters showed her miniatures and daguerreotypes of male family members, but the woman said none matched the description of the man she had seen. Then they remembered the faded photograph of Dr. Blow which hung in a bedroom. When they showed this to the woman, she cried out, "That is the man!"

Dr. Richard Blow had died in that same room — on September 20, 1855!

CHAPTER 27

The Girl Who Was "Born to See"

She was," says Gabrielle Bielenstein, " 'born to see'. Isn't that a marvelous expression? It means, of course, that a person is psychic. Some people are born with perfect pitch, and some can play the piano by ear. She was 'born to see'."

Gabrielle is talking — in the darkened, high-ceilinged parlor of her magnificent Art Nouveau home at 328 Court Street in Olde Towne Portsmouth — about the teenage black girl who worked for Gabrielle's mother nearly half a century ago.

It is called the Maupin House, the family name, and it was built in 1885 because Gabrielle's grandmother, Edmonia, wanted to live on Court Street since it was the most fashionable section of the city. And it was erected on the last available lot in that section of Portsmouth, over a creek bed. The house has "20-odd rooms, including six bathrooms," a beautiful spiral staircase, exquisite wood paneling throughout, and was built at a cost of the then-princely sum of $7,000. Behind it was a splendid walled garden which was a showpiece of the area.

Gabrielle and her identical twin sister, Florence Mary Maupin, grew up in these fashionable surroundings, and the young girl came to work there in the early 1940s, during World War II, when most of the other servants had gone to work in the Norfolk Naval Shipyard nearby.

Almost immediately, she began to "see" things others didn't. "There had been some strange occurrences in the house before," says Gabrielle, "but we had never paid much attention to them. One would hear tales. Some of the other servants would talk occasionally about a rocking chair rocking on the front porch. We would hear noises that sounded like someone descending the staircase. Things like that."

But the new young girl, whose name escapes Gabrielle, saw, felt, and sensed presences in and around the house almost from the day she began work there. And, with uncanny accuracy, they perfectly fit descriptions of past residents, both

157

animal and human.

Consider, for example, the instances of the buried pit bulls. "My mother, Florence, had about given up on having any children, before my sister and I came along, so she had a number of pit bull dogs," Gabrielle says. "Now you have to understand, this was at a time when these dogs were very rare. Few people knew what they looked like. They hadn't got all the notice they have in recent years.

"But my mother didn't have much luck with them. Most

of them died very young, and they were all buried in little pine coffins in a corner of the yard. When the young girl came to work for us, there hadn't been any pit bulls around for years, and I don't believe she had any way of knowing what they looked like. Yet, she told us she saw the dogs playing in the yard. When she was asked to describe what they looked like, she said they were just like Miss Julia's dog. Miss Julia was a neighbor who had a Boston Terrier, which closely resembles the pit bull. How did she know what those dogs looked like unless she saw them?"

The girl also saw the apparition of Miles Portlock. Born a slave before the Civil War, he had been a servant to Gabrielle's great grandmother. "We considered him a part of the family,

and as a child, I can remember him sitting at the kitchen table and drinking ice tea. Someone had given him a gold or silver-headed cane and he used to use it to dig out the grass that grew between bricks. When I was a little girl, he was so old then that this was about all he could do."

Gabrielle says he died about 1939 or 1940 somewhere around the age of 90, well before the girl came to Maupin House to work. Yet she said she saw him in the garden with his cane, and she described him perfectly, too.

And then there were the sightings of Miss Edmonia, Gabrielle's grandmother. The girl said she saw an "old woman" on the staircase at times. "We had a lot of photos in the house in those days," Gabrielle notes, "but there were no recent photos of Edmonia before her death, because she refused to have any taken after she reached middle age. She had been a beautiful woman.

"We took the girl around to view all the photos, and she immediately picked out an earlier portrait of Edmonia, and said that was who she saw. She said it was the same person, only she was much older now. How did she know? How did she pick that one picture out of all the ones in the house. She had no way of knowing what Edmonia looked like. I can't explain it, other than she was born to see!"

The girl only worked at the house for a short period. Her psychic ability unnerved the other servants and they demanded that she leave. In the intervening years there have been a few other haunting occurrences. Gabrielle's husband, Hans, a native of Estonia who now teaches Chinese at Columbia University in New York once woke up in an upstairs bedroom and saw the apparition of a woman appear at an open door.

"They're still here," says current house sitter Emily Mossberger of the ghosts. "They are friendly, but strange things go on." Her daughter was taking a nap one day in a room on the third floor when she was awakened by "something" that was moving her bed. It kept moving as she sat up.

The Maupin House is one of the most popular ones on the annual Olde Towne Ghost Walk at Halloween. Either an actor or a local resident usually plays the part of old Miles Portlock and tells the story of the ghostly legends, and the young girl who was "born to see".

CHAPTER 28

The "Non-Ghosts" of Thoroughgood House

he question is, really, is the Adam Thoroughgood House haunted?

"Definitely not!" says Alice Tripp, an historical interpreter who has worked at the house for the past several years.

"It was haunted even before it was opened to the public," declares Mrs. Martha Lindemann Bradley, the first curator at the house.

"Oh, you might hear a creak or a strange noise from time to time, after all it is a very old house and you should suspect that. But I have not experienced anything out of the ordinary in my years here," adds Nancy Baker, another current historical interpreter.

"I can tell you for a fact there is a ghost there, because I personally experienced its presence once and it scared the life out of me," states Cindy Tatum, who once worked a summer at the house while she was attending college.

And so the argument continues. Present-day hostesses, to the lady, contend there is nothing to the legend, while others, who worked there or visited it as recently as the 1970s swear by their testimony that there is, or was, some spectral phenomenon associated with the house.

What no one disagrees with is that Adam Thoroughgood, and his house, are both interesting in their own right. Captain Adam arrived in the Virginia Colony in 1621 as an indentured servant. He worked hard and did well. By 1626, he had purchased 150 acres of land on the Southampton River.

For his recruitment of 105 new settlers, in 1635, he was awarded 5,350 acres of land along the western shore of the Lynnhaven River. That Thoroughgood was a prominent citizen is also agreed. He was named one of the original eight commissioners of Elizabeth City County, the shire from which New Norfolk and eventually Princess Anne was formed. He also was a burgess, and a member of the governor's council.

There are, however, differing accounts as to actually when

161

the house — said to be the oldest brick house in America — was constructed. Some authors have estimated he built it as early as 1636, three years before he died. But according to the fact sheet visitors are given today, the house was probably built by one of the Thoroughgood descendants about 1680.

It is a one and a half story structure made of brick and oyster shell mortar, with huge chimneys at each end. In an inventory made by Adam's grandson, Argoll Thoroughgood, the house is listed as having hall, parlor, parlor chamber, kitchen, porch chamber, passage and milk house "in ye sellar". In restoration processes, sections of the walls were left exposed inside so visitors may see the mortar and the mortised and pegged rafters. Second story windows are in gable ends only, on both sides of the chimneys. A formal garden with oyster shell walkways separates the house from the Lynnhaven River.

It was sometime after the last major restoration, in 1957, that the ghostly manifestations began to surface.

Charles Thomas Cayce, grandson of the great psychic, Edgar Cayce, and now head of the Association for Research and Enlightenment in Virginia Beach, says the A.R.E. has received calls at times about "strange experiences" at the Thoroughgood House, particularly in an upstairs bedroom. "They were curious, but didn't necessarily want to publicize it," he notes.

He adds that his father, Hugh Lynn Cayce, and a physician friend of his once went to the house to look into some of the reported happenings. "A lady there told them of seeing things fly off of shelves, of little glass objects falling to the floor, and of furniture being moved around when no one was in the house," Cayce says.

Mrs. Bradley says old timers in the area told her of seeing a woman standing in the window with a lighted candle before the house was opened to the public. After it opened, she and other tour guides experienced all sorts of unexplained activities.

As she showed the house to a party including the wife of the ambassador of Denmark, Mrs. Bradley is quoted as saying, "All of us saw a candlestick actually move." She adds that children in particular reported the sighting of a small man in a brown suit. A lawyer visiting from Texas also claimed to have seen an oddly dressed little man. "Children became very restless in the house," Mrs. Bradley adds.

And there was other apparent poltergeist-type movement. Windows mysteriously opened and closed when no one was standing nearby. Tapes recorded in the house turned out blank. Once, in front of about 30 tourists, four glass domes protecting Christmas candles suddenly levitated and crashed to the floor. Such actions brought in newspaper reporters, some of whom said they experienced "things".

The person possibly most affected by all this was Mrs. Tatum, now a telecommunications coordinator in Williamsburg. She worked at the house, giving tours, in 1972, when she was 17.

Cindy says there are a lot of stories about the place which are not told during tours. One is that it may well have been the first house of ill repute in the United States. "After all," she says, "it is on Pleasure House Road." She also tells of the resident who shot himself in the head halfway up the stairwell sometime in the 1700s. "We never talked about that to visitors, but it may be his ghost which came back," Cindy adds. "Actually, there was more than one violent death in the house. A psychic came through one day and said she sensed an unhappy trapped spirit."

Cindy says that when she worked there, the curator told her they had a few spiritual readings and table tappings in the evenings, and at times the table would rock violently. On

Wooden owl at Thoroughgood House allegedly wards off evil spirits.

another occasion during that eventful summer, she recalls coming in one morning and the hostesses found all the upstairs furniture pushed up against the walls, as if someone had cleared the room for a dance. "There were some heavy pieces of furniture, too. We couldn't even move them." Cindy also tells of inexplicable cold drafts on one side of the kitchen during the July heat, and of rush lamps which would "singe up" without being lit.

But the occurrence that convinced her beyond doubt that

there was a presence in the house took place just before closing late one afternoon as she took a group of about 15 visitors to the master bedroom upstairs. "I was standing inside the doorway with my back to the room, talking to the group," she remembers, as distinctly as if it happened yesterday. "All of a sudden several of the women started screaming, and then they began running down the stairs. I turned around and you could see the bed being depressed, as if someone were sitting or lying down on it. This is the truth. There was a definite indentation at least a foot deep!

"I began screaming, too. We all ran outside and we closed the house for the day. A couple of the women later said they saw a vision of a small man on the bed. I didn't see that, but I did see the impression being made. I became hysterical. It really upset me. I'll never forget it as long as I live. My father, who is a minister, didn't want me to go back to the house. He said you don't mess with demons!"

CHAPTER 29

In visions of the dark

night I have dreamed of

joy departed

(*A Dream*)

An Obsession Named Melanie

ary Bowman is a vivacious, red-haired, admitted workaholic who, along with her partner, Kay Buchanan, runs a successful interior design business called "Mary and Me" in Virginia Beach.

Mary Bowman also is, in her words, "metaphysical".

There are, of course, many definitions for this. One is supernatural. Another is relating to the transcendent or super-sensitive, or, if you prefer, a division of philosophy that includes ontology and cosmology. Ontology, in turn, is a branch of metaphysics relating to the nature and relations of being. It also is a particular theory about the nature of being or the kinds of existence. Cosmology is a branch of metaphysics that deals with the universe as an orderly system.

To Mary, however, metaphysical simply means "open". "If you are open," she says, "you go beyond the five senses, which are earth-bound." The lay person would probably call Mary psychic, and she probably would not disagree. She has had a special sensitivity since childhood. When she was 10, for instance, she had a vivid dream in which her grandfather died. She awoke and told her parents. They told her to go back to sleep. An hour later the telephone rang and the family was informed of the grandfather's death. She also once was "visited" by her grandson, in the form of an apparition, a year before he was born!

"Oh yes, I've had some experiences over the years," Mary

smiles. But nothing in the conscious or metaphysical world prepared her for what happened in the fall of 1985. After working late at her office one night, which is most often the case, she got in her car and headed home. As she was driving past the old John B. Dey farm on Greatneck Road, she felt a strange sensation. "There was a voice," she remembers. "It was a girl's voice, and it was crying out for help."

It was not unusual for Mary to receive such a message. She often "reads" the troubled thoughts of others in daily contacts with people, and has had to learn how to turn off such waves. "Otherwise you would be depressed all the time, and I have enough troubles of my own. I can't take on the burdens of the world," she says. But the girl's voice was different. It sounded urgent, and it seemed like she had singled out Mary for a specific purpose.

As time went on, the sensation grew stronger. Each time she drove past that section of the city, she would hear the voice calling out. Mary began to form a mental image. "It scared me at first," she says, "because she looked so much like my own daughter. I saw a picture of a young girl, maybe 18 or 19, or perhaps a little older. She had long blonde hair. She was lying down, as if she were in a coffin. She appeared to be wearing Colonial-era clothes. She had billowing sleeves, and I got the feeling that she lived 200 years ago."

There were other distinct features in Mary's picture. She envisioned a big, meandering farm house with a large porch in white lattice work, part of which was broken. And very distinct in the image was a brick wall. Somehow, Mary felt, all these things were connected. "I became obsessed with it," Mary says. "I took off from my work in the middle of the day and would drive around looking for the house and brick wall. Things got crazy. I had to find out about the girl. Who was she? What did she want? Why was she calling to me? I became a nervous wreck."

Mary went to a well-known psychic counselor in Virginia Beach, but that proved inconclusive. She then was referred to Kay Buchanan who also was psychically gifted. "Kay immediately identified with me," Mary says. "She saw the same thing I did. We felt the name of the girl was Melanie, and that she might have been a school teacher. She had an affair with a married man and had gotten pregnant. We sensed that her lover had killed her, and hastily buried her in an unmarked grave."

It was at this point that Mary says she had to let go. "I wanted to help, but it had become so overpowering I was afraid the search for Melanie would consume me." For the next several months, Mary went about her life, blocking out the vision.

Then one day, as she was out in the area of the old Dey farm on a business call, she saw it. The wall. The brick wall just as she had visualized it. It surrounded the farm house, separating it from the rows of new houses that were being developed all around.

Mary went up to the door of the farmhouse and knocked. When the owner answered, she told him the story of her obsessive dream from start to finish, including the brick wall. "I was afraid he would think I had escaped from the mental ward, but he hardly seemed surprised. In fact, he just said, 'I've got something to show you.' He led me into the garage, and there was a pile of human bones. He said the developers had unearthed about three or four unmarked graves in their diggings, and he had rescued the remains and was going to have them reburied.

"Everything became clear to me all of a sudden. *That* was why Melanie had been calling to me for help," Mary says. "Her resting place had been disturbed. She had been trying to tell me that. Kay and I believe she might even have been worried that people would find out she was pregnant. I don't know for sure."

She must have found peace at last with her reburial. And with it, Mary, too, felt a tremendous relief. The vision and the voice disappeared.

The (Not So) Wicked Witch of Pungo

race Sherwood was not a ghost, and this is not a ghost story.

It is included here more because it is a colorful folklorian tale that is so bizarre it is worthy of the retelling in its own right, and better still, it happens to be true.

Grace Sherwood, you see, was a witch. Or, to be more precise, she often was accused of being a witch. Such accusations, brought about in the post-hysteria of the Salem trials in Massachusetts, and amid a superstition-crazed populace, led her to ignoble humiliation, and, for a time, imprisonment. Fortunately, for Grace and for the conscience of all Tidewater Virginia, they did not lead to a public hanging. She was eventually freed to live out her life in relative quiet. Her legend, however, has survived the centuries and has been richly embellished over the years.

The threat of witchcraft ran rampant through Princess Anne County in the 1690s. It seemed that whenever a farmer's cow died unexpectedly, or a crop failed, the devil was to be blamed, and there was a prevailing opinion that Satan did his dark deeds through real-life witches.

No one knows how or why Grace Sherwood was singled out as being a bearer of such tragic events, but she was. She was a hard working woman, the wife of a carpenter, and the mother of three sons raised in Virginia Beach. Perhaps she was a particularly ugly woman, or outspoken, or just plain unlikable, or all three.

Whatever, official court records indicate she was first brought up on the charge of being a witch on March 3, 1697. But when she and her husband counter sued for defamation of character against her accusers, the affair was settled out of court.

Less than a year and a half later, Grace was back on trial again, and she fought back with a fierce determination. The record tells this story: "At a court held the 10th of September

1698, James Sherwood and Grace his wife suing John Gisbourne and Jane his wife in an action of slander, setting forth by his petition that the defendant had wronged, defamed and abused the said Grace in her good name and reputation saying that she is a witch and bewitched their cotton and prays judgment." The jury didn't take long to rule in Grace's favor.

The accusations, however, had a distinctly negative effect on her reputation, and soon after there was another suit and counter suit with the charges bordering on the ridiculous. This time the accuser was an Elizabeth Barnes. She said Grace stole into her room in the dead of night, jumped over her bed and "rode and whipped" her to the point where she was so scared she couldn't make a sound. If Mrs. Barnes had any lingering doubts about dealing with a witch, they were dispelled with the way Grace exited the room. "She went out of the key hole or a crack in the door like a black cat!," Mrs. Barnes told the court. After four days of trial, this case, too, was dismissed.

Grace next appeared in the records in 1705 when she brought suit against one Elizabeth Hill for having "assaulted, bruised, maimed and barbarously" beaten her because she had allegedly put a hex on Mrs. Hill. Grace asked for an award

of 50 pounds for the offense. Although the justices ruled in her favor, they granted her only 20 shillings.

Even this was too much for the Hills to take, so consequently they filed a formal charge of witchcraft against Grace. And here, the much harassed housewife, now a widow, made a tactical error. She failed to appear for the trial, and the sheriff was ordered to "attach her body" to answer the charges at the next session of court.

Further, it was decreed that she be searched by a jury of women for "any tell-tale marks on her body" which would indicate that she was indeed a witch. It should be explained that in those unenlightened days it was thought that the special mark of a witch was commonly a third pap or "teat" in an abnormal position on a woman's body. This was said to be withered and senseless except when sucked by the Devil. In 1705, the Rev. John Bell of Gladsmuir explained, "This mark is sometimes like a little Teate; sometimes like a bluish spot; and I myself have seen it on the body of a confessing Witch like a little power mark of a bleak color, somewhat hard, and withal insensible, so as it did not bleed when I pricked it."

Grace consented to the search. On March 7, 1706, a jury of 12 women, which the aforementioned Elizabeth Barnes as forewoman, reported to the justices that it had found "Two things like titts with Several other Spotts." This apparently threw the learned judges into utter confusion. Nothing like this had ever happened before. With the deftness of politicians, they referred the case to the Royal Governor and Council and the Attorney General of the Virginia Colony in Williamsburg. They threw it right back to Princess Anne County.

On May 2, Grace was ordered to be held in lieu of bond, and the sheriff was instructed to search her house "and all Suspicious places Carefully for all Images & Such like things as may any way Strengthen the Suspicion." Next, she was ordered to be searched again for suspicious marks on her body, but this time a panel of jury women couldn't be assembled. Many by now didn't believe that she was guilty and refused to take part even under the threat of being held in contempt of court. Some were terrified.

As more or less a last resort, the court said that Grace "should be tried in ye water by Ducking". The quaint belief then was that if you tied up a suspected witch with a rope secured around her right thumb and left big toe and left thumb and right big toe and threw her into a body of water and she swam or floated, she was indeed a witch. If she sank, she was not, and if she was lucky she would be pulled from the water before drowning. Again, Grace consented to the test, probably because she was tired of the whole sordid episode.

The trial by water was delayed once because, of all things, it was too rainy on the day of the first attempt. Some said it was the Devil who caused this postponement. Finally, on July 10, 1706, at 10 a.m., Grace was trussed up in the appropriate manner and readied for her dunking in the Lynnhaven River. The event apparently was well attended by hundreds of the curious.

Somehow, Grace survived. She did not sink. Amid a loud chorus of cheers and jeers, she bobbed to the top of the water. In this most curious fashion she was thus adjudged as being a witch. Afterwards, five courageous and "antient weomen" searched her body again and declared on oath that she "is not like ym nor noe other woman yt they knew of having two things like titts on her private parts of a Black Coller being Blacker yn ye Rest of her Body."

Armed with such irrefutable evidence, the justices ordered the sheriff to commit her to the Common Gaol of the County and "there to secure her by irons." How long she remained in jail has been lost in time, but apparently she was dismissed and sent home within a relatively short period to live out her life with what dignity she could muster. The court records show no further mention of Grace Sherwood until she made

out her will in 1733. She died seven years later.

There have been many preposterous legends associated with Grace over the past 300 years, but none are really needed. The true story of her real-life ordeal is strange enough in itself. It is also the reason why Witch Duck Road in Virginia Beach today is known as Witch Duck Road.

CHAPTER 31

He might not sing

so wildly well

A mortal melody

(Israfel)

A Haunting Love Story

he house in the Laurel Cove section of Virginia Beach has been a hotbed of psychic activity ever since Bee and her husband moved into it in 1972. (For personal reasons soon to be evident, the woman's full name, and the names of others involved here have been abbreviated.)

A great range of manifestations have occurred, and still do. In fact, says Bee today, "the house is absolutely alive with ghosts. I've heard the sound of footfalls on the stairs. There are moaning voices, and a woman giggling. You sometimes hear someone humming. There is the distinct noise of a rustling skirt. Doors open and close with no one there. An expensive jade vase was knocked off the mantel, and pictures have fallen off the walls."

Bee is not alone in having experienced the occurrences. Her husband, and a number of her friends have also witnessed the spectral happenings. "Our bed has been shaken and slapped on occasion," she continues. "Once we heard the sounds of a gala party going on downstairs at 2 a.m. When we went down to investigate, all was quiet. Another time, we had our own New Year's Eve party to beat all New Year's Eve parties! A meatball leaped four feet in the air out of its chafing dish. And a guest had his plate of food whisked from his lap. It fell on the floor but no food was spilled. At a card party once, one of my guests had her tea cup stand on its own at a 90 degree angle, yet no tea spilled."

Some of the strangest events have involved the many mirrors Bee has placed throughout the house. Once she awoke to find the distinct handprints and footprints of a baby clearly outlined on a large mirror. One of the footprints had six toes! A newsman photographed the images, and although the results are blurred and inconclusive, he himself had no doubts of what he had seen.

At various times the house has been filled with odd odors, including those of fudge cooking, and of tomato sauce. Bee also has seen the apparition of a small girl, "with long hair and a protuberant stomach," looking at her clothes in the bedroom closet. The ghostly phenomena have been so consistently prevalent that several newspaper and magazine articles have been written about them.

Bee, who says she has been "intuitive" all her life, believes the manifestations are directly related to the history of the area. The development is built on the site of the Eastwood Plantation, which dates back to 1637. "There are a number of desecrated graves right in this vicinity," she points out. "There are at least six graves and one tombstone just across the street. There may be more directly under the house."

Once, Bee hosted a seance in her home, with nine guests present. An experienced medium conducted it. In a trance, she assumed the voice of a young girl and shouted, "They wouldn't listen to me. I'm dead!" The question was posed, "How did you die," and voice responded, "I don't know. I don't know. I don't know" The "girl" was identified as a Rosemary Savage, but when the medium came out the trance-state, she had no knowledge of what she had proclaimed. She said only, "I was not in control. I feel so drained."

Subsequently, Bee had a vivid dream about a young girl in an 18th century schoolhouse, and her teacher had warned that she was about to die. On her way home, the girl was tragically killed in an accident. Bee is convinced that the girl in her dream was none other than Rosemary Savage. She has researched the name and all indications are that there was such a girl who had died accidentally more than 200 years ago.

But as interesting and as unusual as all that has gone on in the house has been, it merely serves as a prelude to the incredible story of Bee's long-term life and death relationship with a gentleman we shall call Bill.

He was tall — about six foot five — charming, debonair,

generous and charismatic. He seemed to have been everywhere and done everything. He had been a friend of Al Capone. He had been involved in the development of fuel for diesel engines. He had been in the silent movies. He had married a millionairess. He was the epitome of social grace and courtly manners. He had an imposing personality. Everyone liked him.

From the moment Bee met him, she was mesmerized. And Bill fell immediately and irretrievably in love with her. The problem was, each still had a spouse. Bill nevertheless openly professed his love to Bee, and then even to her husband. Bee told Bill she would not leave her husband. Bill then decided that the next best thing would be to spend as much time in Bee's company as possible.

From then on, for the next two or three years, the four of them — Bee and her husband, and Bill and his wife — were almost inseparable. "It was a whirlwind relationship," she recalls. "Every Thursday we would go out for Chinese food. Every Friday it would be the Yacht Club. Every Saturday the Harbor Club. And every Sunday, brunch somewhere. Through it all, my husband was never jealous. He seemed fascinated by Bill."

The four went on trips together — to New York for a lavish stay at the Plaza Hotel; to the islands for holidays in the sun. Bill picked up the bills. He sent Bee flowers; garlands of flowers. He feted her at a massive cocktail party he once threw in Williamsburg. He offered her a six carat diamond ring if she would leave her husband. But she remained faithful.

Then Bill got cancer. As his condition worsened, Bee spent more and more time with him. They talked endlessly about life, death and the hereafter. He told her that he believed the mind goes on living even after the body expires. He said he called it the mind. Some people called it the soul. He told her that if there was any way for him to communicate with her after he died, he would find it. "We shed our astral bodies," he said, "but our minds go on." Bee told him she would try to be receptive. He died in October 1982.

Some time later — Bee doesn't remember exactly when — she began writing down details of their relationship in long-hand. She felt that Bill was so colorful, and their love had been so special, that it would make a good book, and possibly a movie. One day she was reading her rough notes onto a tape recorder, trying to dictate them in paragraph form. She finished one passage and then hesitated, trying to recall just what had happened next. There was a pause on the tape. Then she went on.

In playing back the tape, when she got to the part where she had paused, she gasped. On the tape was a man's deep voice filling in the blanks in her memory. It was Bill's voice! Frightened, Bee grabbed her car keys and ran out the front door. She didn't come back for hours.

Later, she had the tape analyzed by experts. They couldn't explain it. In time, Bill's voice began appearing on other tapes. Once Bee was singing at the piano with her sister. Bee had long ago been a singer at a French nightclub on Long Island. When she played that tape back, Bill's voice came through loud, if not clear, singing "There Is A Place For Us." Bee and her sister were astonished. The male voice is deep and raspy, and it sounds like record that is being played at half speed. The voice kind of drags and shakes. It is, to say the least, an eerie sound.

There are other manifestations of Bill's return, too. "He used to smoke expensive, imported cigars," Bee says. "They had a marvelous aroma about them. I used to love them. That's one way I know he's around today. I can smell the same aroma." Another way she can sense his presence is through her tiny dog, Brandy — half Chihuahua and half Beagle. "He sees Bill," she says. "I see Brandy's eyes follow him across the living room until he sits down in his favorite chair."

At other times, Bee has had her hair stroked by a mystery hand. "Once I looked in the mirror when this happened, and I could see my hair move," she says. At one point, she called a psychic couple and had them visit her in the house to offer advice. The woman saw Bill's vision sitting in his chair. She described him perfectly to Bee although she had no prior knowledge of what he looked like. The woman's husband advised Bee to establish a set means of communicating with Bill. He suggested having the ghost turn the light switch to one room on and off as a signal. Bee says this is how she knows Bill is around now.

"I feel like we are soul mates," she says. "He had so much empathy, so much feeling and sensitivity for me. He loved me so much he wanted to share it in life after death."

* * * * *

hostly voices on tape are not a new phenomenon. There was documented evidence of their appearance as early as 1959. At that time a celebrated Swedish painter, musician and film producer named Friedrich Jurgenson took his battery operated tape recorder out into a remote part of the countryside near his villa to record bird songs. When he played the tape back later, Jurgenson found not only bird sounds, but faint human voices, speaking in Swedish and Norwegian, and discussing nocturnal bird songs.

178

At first he thought he might have picked up a stray radio transmission by chance. However, when he repeated the experiment he heard further voices, this time addressing him personally and claiming to be dead relatives and friends of his! Jurgenson amassed more evidence over the next several years and wrote a book titled "Voices from the Universe," in 1964.

The book led to further scientific study of the phenomenon. One team of experts was organized by the eminent German psychologist, Professor Hans Bender, director of the government-funded parapsychological research unit at the University of Freiburg. It repeated the experiments and analyzed the results. The team's startling findings, as reported in the 1984 book, "Survival of Death," were summarized as follows: that under differing conditions and circumstances a factory-clean tape, run through an ordinary tape recording head in an otherwise silent environment, will contain human voices speaking recognizable words when played back; that the origin of these voices is apparently inexplicable in the light of present day science; and that the voices themselves are objective in that they yield prints in the same way as normal voices, and register as visible oscillograph impulses on videotape recordings. Dr. Bender considered these "voices from nowhere" to be of tremendous importance, representing a significant whole new field in the study of the paranormal.

* * * * *

One prominent international figure who firmly believed that voice contact could be made with those who had died was Thomas Alva Edison, the famous American inventor. In fact, he felt so strongly about this issue that he worked on developing a machine to facilitate the conversation, but he was unsuccessful.

In an interview with Scientific American Magazine, published in October 1920, Edison expressed his views on the subject as follows: "If our personality survives, then it is strictly logical and scientific to assume that it retains memory, intellect and other faculties and knowledge that were acquired in this earth. Therefore, if personality exists after what we call death, it is reasonable to conclude that those who leave this earth would like to communicate with those they have left here . . . I am inclined to believe that our personality hereafter will

179

be able to affect matter. If this reasoning be correct, then, if we can evolve an instrument so delicate as to be affected, or moved, or manipulated . . . by our personality as it survives in the next life, such an instrument, when made available, ought to record something."

The Impish Prankster at Pine Tree Inn

he next time you're in the mood for a nice quiet candlelight dinner, with outstanding ambiance and service, and superb cuisine, you might want to try Tandom's Pine Tree Inn on Virginia Beach Boulevard. You may even catch a glimpse of a puckish female ghost who is said to have been seen in the ladies' rest room, the linen closet, the kitchen and elsewhere from time to time. Often, "she" seems to enjoy playing mischievous little tricks on waitresses and kitchen help, but on occasion she also has appeared to diners.

Tandom's is one of the oldest — and finest — restaurants in Virginia Beach. Its veal, chicken and seafood dishes all are expertly prepared and many people have eaten there regularly for years, the most telling testament of all. It has been operating since 1927, and was a roadside stopover before that. There are tales that, during prohibition, high stakes poker games took place in a back room; bring your own bottle. According to one of the legends, a fashionable lady held her own in the card games until one day when a gentleman, who either caught her cheating, or just couldn't stand being beaten by a woman, allegedly shot her.

Whether or not this really happened has been long lost in the mists of time. The episode could not be factually verified. Still, one might wonder about it when the experience of Whitney Elliot is considered. Whitney is a bright, young entrepreneur who runs her own marketing business in Virginia Beach. She dined with a friend of hers at the Pine Tree Inn one evening in the winter of 1989-1990. It was late and there were only a few people in the restaurant, when Whitney went to the powder room.

She tells what happened next: "There are three stalls, and I always look under the stalls before I enter one. I saw a woman's feet under one of them, but the strange thing was, she was wearing real old shoes. They were the high button type with laces all the way up, like, you know, from another era, maybe the 1920s. I also heard a rustling sound, like an old time skirt.

"Weird, I thought, but I went into a stall opposite from where I saw the shoes. Now, no one else came into the room while I was there, and I didn't hear any other noises, especially of the door to the outer room opening or closing. There was no water running, no flushing or anything. Yet when I left, there was no one in the room! I looked under the stalls again, and the shoes were gone. I know that no one could have left without me hearing it.

"I went back to my table and told my friend. We called the waitress over and when I asked her if they had a ghost in the restaurant, I thought she would faint. She turned as white as a sheet. She told us we were not the first to have such an experience; that, in fact, many things had happened to her. She told us, for instance, that she had the late shift one night. They close at 10 p.m. on weekends, but if someone comes in just before 10, it can be around midnight before she leaves. One of the last things she has to do when closing up is blow out all the candles on the tables, maybe 25 or 30 of them.

"She said she blew out the candles and went into the kitchen. A few minutes later one of the managers came in and asked her why she hadn't blown out the candles. She went back into the dining room to look. They were all lit! She said the hair on the back of her neck and arms stood up. She also told us that whatever the presence was, it was often felt in the old linen closet and that she would never go in there by herself. She added that she could always tell when the ghost was there. She could feel it. She had gone into the kitchen earlier and told the cooks, but they said no, 'she' wasn't in the dining room, 'she' was out in the fish house, because the door there had been opening and closing by itself that night. 'She' apparently knows her way around quite well.

"I can tell you this," Whitney concluded. "I know what I saw, and it wasn't something alive!"

One person who is convinced something or someone roams through the restaurant in the night and early morning hours is Angie Reitzel who has baked fresh breads and served as a prep cook and in other roles for nearly 20 years. "I've heard plenty of stories over the time I've been here — from waiters,

182

waitresses, dishwashers, cooks, you name it. And I've had a number of things happen to me personally that I could not explain."

Take, for example, the incident of the missing coffee. Angie arrives in the morning very early to do her baking, often while it still is dark outside. On this particular day, one of the managers came in and she asked him if he wanted a cup of coffee. Sure. "I made a pot and poured two cups full on the counter," she remembers, as if it had happened yesterday. "Then I turned around and went to get some sugar and cream, maybe five or 10 feet away. When I went back the coffee was gone! I said to myself, 'Am I crazy? I thought I just poured two cups.' Then I looked into the bottom of the cups and there was still a few drops of coffee left in them. I had gotten the cups clean from the cupboard. They had been stacked upside down. And the manager wasn't even in the kitchen. How do you explain that?"

Another time, a few years ago, Angie and a friend of hers were at the restaurant one night when it was closed. They were preparing food for a Christmas party for Pine Tree Inn personnel which was being held at another location. "We took off our coats and started to work," she says. "Then we heard some pots and pans rattling, and we thought my friend's husband had come in to help us. We looked around, but there was no one there. We forgot about it.

"When we finished, we packed up the food, put on our coats and started to leave. The doorway had long plastic flaps hanging down, and as we approached it, the flaps parted. They opened up as if someone were holding them for us! My friend screamed. She said she wasn't going through there. I had to talk to her for a long time before I could get her to go through the doorway."

Angie says there have been many other manifestations over the years. Lights that apparently burn out at night burn brightly the next morning. The dishwasher, a big commercial one with "all kinds of switches", occasionally turns on and off by itself. Once, a waiter brought a tray of drinks to a table, then put them down and turned to get a cup of coffee. When he turned back, the drinks had vanished. At other times, matches seem to fly about inexplicably.

Angie says a lot of psychic activity is associated with the linen closet. "The lights go on and off in there all the time. Employees turn out the lights when we are locking up, and then they just go on again. This has even happened to the managers. One night one of them turned out the lights in the linen closet. He was sure of it. Then, in the parking lot he saw the light on in there," she says.

Angie thinks the ghost could be the spirit of a young girl who once worked as a bus girl at the restaurant, but died a tragic death. "Maybe she enjoyed working there and just comes back to visit. Who knows?" Angie asks. "The first time you hear or see something, you don't want to believe it. You shrug it off. But then you begin to wonder. So many things have happened."

Angie even saw the ghost once. "It was early," she recalls, "about 7:30 in the morning. I was at a mixing bowl preparing muffins. There was just me and one cook there. I looked over and saw this person sorting silverware. I couldn't tell if it was a boy or girl. I only knew he or she was young and had short hair. I thought maybe it was the new dishwasher. He comes in at 8.

"I asked him to get me some trash cans, but there was no response. I said, 'this kid didn't hear me, or he or she just didn't want to get the cans.' I tried again and there was no reply. I could see the person through and around a big stack of glasses.

"So I went over to where he or she was standing and when I got there he or she had disappeared. I couldn't figure it out. I went into the kitchen and asked the cook where the dishwasher had gone. He said he hadn't seen anyone. So I went through the dining room. I looked in the storage room, the linen room and both bathrooms. There was no one anywhere. Finally, I went out back and opened the door. The guy who opens our oysters was out there and I asked him. He said he hadn't seen anyone come in or out. They all thought I was crazy! But I saw it and it definitely was a real person. It wasn't an indistinct image or anything like that."

And so the mystery remains unsolved. Angie and others say the spirit seems to come and go at random. Nothing will happen for weeks at a time, and then, suddenly, the visitor is back. Is it the young bus girl, or is it the lady with the high button shoes from a time long ago? Or is it both?

Whatever, it is not a hostile spirit, but one who apparently has a prankish sense of humor. It seems to add an extra dimension to dining at Tandom's Pine Tree Inn.

The Ghosts of Edgar Cayce

I t would seem almost sacrilegious to write a book on the Ghosts of Tidewater and not include at least some mention — if not a chapter or entire section — on the extraordinary man from Virginia Beach who is widely recognized as perhaps the greatest psychic of the 20th century — Edgar Cayce.

He was also known as the "Sleeping Prophet," the "Psychic Diagnostician," and the "Miracle Worker of Virginia Beach." For more than 40 years, Cayce helped save lives, lengthen lives, cure ailments, and heal the sick through detailed "readings" he gave while in a trance-like state. Two-thirds of his more than 14,000 readings were medically related. Though he had no more than an eighth grade education, Cayce, while asleep, somehow had the ability to envision and diagnose the ailments, no matter how complicated, of people all over the country. Then, in precise, meticulous, and sophisticated detail, he would prescribe the medicines and/or treatments essential to the patient's return to full health. Often, such prescriptions included lengthy, and complex medical terminology, and, at times, obscure or long forgotten remedies of which Cayce had no knowledge when awake.

Astoundingly, of those cases verified by patients' reports, 85 percent of the diagnoses were found to be completely accurate, and those who followed the prescribed treatments got the results predicted in the readings.

Consider, for example, a couple of sample case studies. In one instance, he gave a reading for a man who had been confined to an insane asylum for three years following a nervous breakdown caused, it had been suspected, by nervous tension. In the reading, Cayce said "through pressures upon nerve energies in the coccyx area and the ileum plexus, as well as that pressure upon the lumbar axis, there had been a deflection of coordination between the sympathetic and the cerebrospinal nervous system." He further diagnosed that the man's condition

had actually been caused by a spinal injury incurred by a fall. He didn't need psychotherapy. Instead, Cayce advised osteopathic adjustment and a mild, specially outlined electrotherapy to normalize the disrupted nerve forces. The treatment was followed and the results were dramatically successful. The man regained excellent health within six months and returned to a normal life.

Cayce's wife, Gertrude, once suffered from what doctors had diagnosed as incurable tuberculosis. He gave her a reading and prescribed a diet, some simple drugs, and an unheard of treatment: inhaling apple brandy fumes from a charred oak keg. Remarkably, it worked, and Mrs. Cayce recovered from her "incurable" tuberculosis.

One of the most amazing cures effected by the readings involved a young girl who had suddenly gone insane. Her condition did not respond to any of the treatments administered at the hospital. In desperation, her parents turned to Cayce for help. In his sleep-state, he described the trouble as an impacted wisdom tooth which was disrupting nerve and brain function. He said when the tooth was removed, the trouble would disappear. He had never seen the girl — he was 400 miles away from the hospital where she was staying — yet when a dentist examined her, the impaction was found exactly as outlined. The dentist removed the tooth. Four hours later the girl had regained her normal state of mind and never again showed any symptoms of mental disturbance.

To further his work for the benefit of mankind — Cayce never really profited in a material sense from his psychic powers — he founded, in 1931, the Association for Research and Enlightenment at 67th Street and Atlantic Avenue in Virginia Beach. Today, the A.R.E., headed by his grandson, Charles Thomas Cayce, has 100,000 members worldwide, and is dedicated to physical, mental and spiritual self-improvement programs through researching and applying the information in Edgar Cayce's psychic readings.

Eventually, in addition to medical diagnoses, the scope of his readings expanded to include information and advice on approximately 10,000 different subjects. These included such topics as world religions, philosophy, psychology, dreams, history, reincarnation, soul growth, diet and nutrition, spiritual development, and the fabled lost continent of Atlantis, among others.

When he died in 1945, Edgar Cayce left behind a legacy of readings which have stood the test of decades of intensive research and study. He remains the most documented psychic of all times.

Did Edgar Cayce ever have any experiences with ghosts? The answer, says Charles Thomas, is yes. "I was only three when my grandfather died, so I can only tell you what I heard from members of the family and friends," he adds. "My father (Hugh Lynn Cayce, now dead) and my uncle (Edgar Evans Cayce, still living in Virginia Beach) mentioned stories about my grandfather communicating with ghosts. Are there such things as ghosts? The answer is yes. Some people are talented or gifted in ways of communicating with spirits. They are psychically talented in the same way a person may be musically or athletically talented."

Vada F. Carlson, in a short composition on the early life of Edgar Cayce titled, "The Vision of the Promise," said that Edgar saw and played with a whole group of ghostly playmates, both boys and girls. "It was disappointing to Edgar," Carlson wrote,, "that the grownups could not see the 'play people' with whom he had so much fun, but Anna Seay, a small girl who lived nearby and sometimes came over to play with him, saw them as well as he did. She and Edgar played happily with them in woodsy places and in the cool shade of the barn. Edgar's mother believed him when he told her about the invisible children . . . . His mother was the one person in the world who completely understood him . . . One day she glanced out the window and saw them waiting in the yard for him. 'Go play with your friends,' she told him. 'They're waiting.' It made Edgar very happy to know that she, too, could see the children."

Cayce, Carlson reported, seemed amazed that his spectral friends could run in the rain without getting wet, and he wondered why they always disappeared whenever grownups came near. Once Edgar was talking and laughing in the field when his father came by and asked him who he was talking to. "My friends," he told him. "Where are they?" asked his father. "Right here," the boy said, pointing. But his father saw no one.

There are two specific references in Edgar Cayce's authorized biography — written by his long-time friend Thomas Sugrue during Cayce's lifetime — relating to ghosts. One involved the death of his grandfather when Edgar was a small boy of five or six. They had been out horseback riding together, Grandpa in front, little Edgar behind him, holding on. They stopped in a pond to water the horse, and the boy slid off. Suddenly, the horse threw up its head, reared, and plunged into deeper water. "We don't really know what happened," says Charles Thomas Cayce today. "Perhaps it was frightened by a snake." The horse swam to the other side of the pond and raced to a fence, failed to jump it, and galloped back to the pond, with Grandpa hanging on.

This time the horse stumbled as it entered the water, and Grandpa was thrown over its head, landing on his back. The horse got to its feet, reared again, and brought the full force of its forefeet down on the old man's chest. Then it ran off. Grandpa's head was under water. Young Edgar called to him and when there was no answer, frightened, he ran for help. But by then it was too late and his grandfather was dead. Edgar said that even at that moment, he could still talk with his grandfather, but in the excitement and the grief, no one listened to him.

Later, Sugrue said in his biography that Edgar would see his grandfather "sometimes in the barns, usually when the tobacco was being fired. Of course, Grandpa wasn't really there. You could see through him if you looked real hard." Edgar would only tell his mother and grandmother about the apparitions, because he knew that at that time it would have angered his father. But his grandmother liked him to tell her about seeing Grandpa.

Once when Edgar came into the house his mother asked him what he had been doing. He told her he was visiting with Grandpa in the tobacco barn. His mother seemed unconcerned, but one of his aunts who was visiting, told him he was a wicked boy. "How can you tell such wicked lies, when you know your grandfather is dead and buried?" she chided. "But I saw him," Edgar pleaded. "I talked to him, and he talked to me." When the aunt scolded Edgar's mother, she merely replied that Edgar was a truthful boy, and that if he said he saw his grandfather, she did not doubt him.

The second reference in the biography to his seeing a presence occurred when Edgar was 12 years old. "When he was young, my grandfather spent a lot of time alone in the fields," says Charles Thomas. He would go out often to read his Bible. One afternoon in May as he sat alone in the woods, reading the story of Manoah, he became aware of the presence of someone else."

Edgar looked up and saw a woman standing before him. At first, peering into the sun after reading, he thought it was his mother. But then she spoke and he realized it was someone he did not know. "Her voice," wrote Sugrue, "was soft and very clear; it reminded him of music." The woman told him his prayers had been answered and she asked him what he would like most of all, so that she might give it to him.

At first, he could not speak. He was frightened, especially when he noticed that she had shadows on her back "shaped like wings." She reassured him by smiling. Finally, he managed to say that, "most of all, I would like to be helpful to others, and especially to children when they are sick." Then, suddenly, the woman was gone.

Edgar ran home and told his mother of the ethereal experience. He told her that maybe he had been reading the Bible too much and was losing his sanity. She reassured him by quoting from the Gospel of St. John. ". . . Verily, verily, I say unto you, Whatsoever ye shall ask the Father in my name, he will give it (to) you. Hitherto have ye asked nothing in my name: ask, and ye shall receive, that your joy may be full." Then she told her son that because he was a good boy and wanted to help others, "why shouldn't your prayers be heard?"

They talked about the meaning of the apparitional visit. It might mean, she told Edgar, that he was destined to become a doctor, or a preacher, or possibly a missionary. Only later, when he became fully aware of his psychic powers, did he realize the true meaning of his experience. It meant that he was to use those powers in a positive way to help others.

And the first true clue to his great gift came the next evening. He had done miserably at school that day, particularly in his spelling lessons. When he couldn't correctly spell the word "cabin", his teacher made him stay after school and write "cabin" 500 times on the blackboard. His father heard about the incident and that night he told Edgar he was a disgrace to the family. After supper the boy and his father sat for hours, poring over the lesson book, and Edgar's answers were all wrong. Twice Squire Cayce had become so exasperated, he had knocked the boy out of his chair.

Then, tired and sleepy, Edgar heard the voice of the woman he had seen the day before. She told him if he could sleep a little, "we can help you." He begged his father to let him rest. He reluctantly agreed, telling him it would be his last chance. The Squire then went into the kitchen for a few minutes and Edgar, almost instantly, nodded off.

When his father came back, Edgar woke up and told him he knew his lessons. And he did. He got every word right. Not only that, he knew the assignment for the next day. In fact, by sleeping on his book, he had, somehow, inexplicably, memorized every word and picture on every page in the book. He could envision the word, where it was on the page, and what the illustrations were. When he spelled "synthesis" perfectly, the Squire lost his temper and struck him again.

When Edgar told his mother about the episode the next day, and still knew every word on every page of the book, she said to him that she was sure the lady was "keeping her promise." After that Edgar would take other school books to bed, put them under his pillow and sleep on them, and the next day he would know everything in the book. When his befuddled father asked him how he did it, he told him he didn't know. But it worked!

Was the lady angel an apparition or a dream? "I'm not sure," says Charles Thomas. "But I was told that it was something he experienced while he was awake, so I don't think it was a dream."

Cayce apparently had a number of encounters with ghosts during his adult years as well, and although this is not specifically addressed in his readings, Charles Thomas says his father, Hugh Lynn Cayce, remembered Edgar talking about such incidents at times. Hugh Lynn, in fact, in a lecture series, told of the gentle tapping one evening at a downstairs window. Edgar rose from his bed to go down and see who it was. Apparently, it was an apparition, because Hugh Lynn wrote: "It seemed to him (Edgar) perfectly natural procedure to get up, go downstairs, unlock the front door and let in a rather diffident young woman who had been quite dead a few years." (Author's underlining.)

The woman told Cayce in so many words that she had died (of toxic throat infection) without fully realizing she was dead, and she was having a terrible time adjusting to "the other side." (Author's quotations.) In this confused state, she had haunted Cayce's former photographic studio in Selma, Alabama, but then, when she found out he had moved to Virginia Beach, she had travelled there to see if he could help her. He did. Hugh Lynn said he taught her how to release herself from what some people call the "earthbound condition," and to move forward in her path of development.

"Edgar Cayce both saw and heard this girl," Hugh Lynn said. "Actually he saw *through* her, because she wasn't exactly solid, but she was solid enough to ask for his help, and to tap on the window loud enough to attract his attention." Hugh Lynn said this was a combination of clairvoyance and clairaudience.

Hugh Lynn himself, along with other members of his family, experienced ghostly visitations once in their house at Virginia Beach shortly after Squire Cayce, Hugh Lynn's grandfather, had died. They heard "puttering around" upstairs, mostly in a bedroom, when there was no one upstairs. Edgar told everyone not to worry, that it was just his father "returning" to straighten out some papers before he "left." Edgar said to just leave him alone and he would be gone pretty soon.

But Hugh Lynn couldn't resist the temptation. "I heard the noise so clearly at lunch," he said later, "that I insisted on running upstairs to check." As he reached the landing before getting to the top of the stairs, he felt a presence which he described as "a cold area . . . a feeling like cobwebs." Hugh Lynn said "every hair stood at attention."

One evening in the fall of 1933, Edgar was alone downstairs in his Virginia Beach house, listening to the radio, when suddenly the room got icy cold, and he felt something "uncanny or unusual" taking place. When Edgar looked toward the radio, he realized that a friend of his who had been dead for several months, was sitting in front of the radio!

Cayce said, "he turned and smiled at me, saying 'There *is* the survival of personality. *I know*! And a life of service and prayer is the only one to live.' I was shaking all over. He said nothing more and just seemed to disappear. I turned off the radio. It still appeared as if the room was full of some presence.

Edgar Cayce   *Photo courtesy of the Association for Research and Enlightenment*

As I switched off the light and climbed the stairs, I could hear many voices coming from the darkened room.

"Jumping in bed and shivering from cold, I aroused my wife. She asked me why I hadn't turned off the radio. I assured her that I had. She opened the door and said, 'I hear it. I hear voices.' We both did."

Cayce wrote of the experience in a short monograph. He noted in it that this particular friend had been an executive of the Western Union Telegraph Company in Chicago, and that when the two of them had gotten together, they often discussed whether or not there was a survival of personality after death. Cayce said the friend would usually close the talk by saying, "Well, whichever one goes first will communicate with the other."

Perhaps the most frightening manifestation occurred in June 1936, on a bright sunny day, when Edgar was hoeing in his garden. He heard a noise he described like "a swarming of bees." Startled, he looked up and saw in the sky a chariot drawn by four white horses. Then he heard a voice saying "look behind you." When he did, he saw a man with a shield and helmet, kneeguards and a cape, clad in burnished silver. The phantom raised his hand in salute and said, "the chariot of the Lord and the horsemen thereof." With that, the vision vanished. Cayce was so upset, he bolted into the house and locked himself in his study. Hours later, when he emerged, he said what he saw signalled the approach of World War II and the death of millions.

There were several other incidents involving ghostly visitations. Cayce seemed to attract them, but many were not officially recorded, and have been lost to memory lapses over the years. Others now are but fragmentary remembrances. Gerry McDowell, a spry septuagenarian who works in the library of the Association for Research and Enlightenment, says she recalls one such occasion, hidden somewhere in the A.R.E.'s voluminous files. Edgar was on a train travelling from Virginia Beach to Hopkinsville, Kentucky, his birthplace. A man sat down next to him and they carried on a conversation for some time. Then the man told Edgar that he had recently drowned at Virginia Beach!

Edgar, who died in 1945, is said to have reappeared at least once, coincidentally to the same Gerry McDowell. It happened in 1976. Gerry at the time was a volunteer worker at A.R.E. She had finished a shift at her full time job, and not feeling tired, had gone out to the old building at 67th and Atlantic Avenue in Virginia Beach to do some work there. But when she kept nodding off, she was told to go outside in the hallway and lie down on the couch. It was the same couch that Edgar had used to sleep on for many of his readings.

"I guess I slept for about an hour," Gerry says. "When I awoke, there, standing over me, was a man. I had never seen Edgar Cayce in life, but I recognized him immediately from his photographs. He was wearing a blue suit, a blue tie and a white shirt. He smiled at me and I smiled at him. He pointed a finger at me, and then he disappeared. I went in and told the others in the office what had happened, and they said it meant he wanted me to stay; that I would never get away from here now." Two years later Gerry joined the full time staff at A.R.E. and has worked there faithfully ever since.

* * * * *

Though Charles Thomas Cayce does not profess to have psychic abilities like his grandfather did, he nevertheless has had his share of psychic experiences. For example, he once dreamed that a plane would crash on its way from Norfolk to Atlanta — and it did! Cayce has a degree in psychology, and when he has the time, he likes to work with and counsel psychically-gifted young people.

One of the most unusual cases he ever encountered occurred several years ago, involving a 14-year-old schoolgirl and her "ghostly friend." "Her name was Phyllis, and she said her unseen friend's name was Phil," Cayce remembers. She told him Phil was with her most of the time and that he had blond hair in a crew cut and had died suddenly. The girl's mother had arranged the appointment because she was understandably concerned about her daughter communicating with a dead person.

Cayce asked to speak with "Phil" but Phyllis told him he couldn't. She was the only one he would "talk" to, and he did it in a strange manner — by writing on her kneecap. Next, Cayce set up an impromptu test. He walked down the hall to another room, opened an 800-page dictionary at random, and then went back and asked Phyllis to ask Phil what page he had opened the book to. Phil wrote the page number on her knee and it was correct. Cayce was amazed. He repeated the test several times, the last time opening the dictionary without looking at the page number, possibly to preclude Phil from reading his mind. The page number was called out accurately every time!

"Whether this was a psychic ability of hers, or there really was the ghost of a person around her, I don't know," Cayce said. "In either event, it was an impressive demonstration. I did learn that Phil had only 'appeared' to her shortly after the death of her grandmother. Phyllis also said she often still saw her grandmother rocking in her favorite rocking chair, but she didn't talk about it because she knew it would upset her father."

Cayce sensed Phyllis was a little uncomfortable about the situation, so he arranged for her to meet some other teenage girls who had psychic sensitivities. After that she felt better about things. Eventually, she lost touch with Phil, which Cayce says is quite common because teens have a great desire to conform. They often try to block out their intuitive abilities.

* * * * *

Another memorable case involved a Virginia Beach teenager who appeared to be haunted by a poltergeist. Objects fell and moved around her with no apparent cause. Her mother brought her to see Cayce after a particularly disturbing incident. The girl and her mother had argued about how late she could stay out at night. As the teenager passed through the kitchen while her mother was preparing dinner, soup jumped out of the pot and all over the mother's clothes, according to the account Cayce heard. Fortunately, the soup was not hot enough to burn her, but the mother was extremely frightened. Cayce believed there was no poltergeist involved. Rather, he suspected, the girl was deeply psychic and was able to move inanimate objects without even being aware she was doing it.

* * * * *

The question is often asked: why did Edgar Cayce choose to live and work in Virginia Beach. The answer, or answers came in a reading he gave more than 65 years ago in Dayton, Ohio. "Actually, there were a couple reasons given in his reading," says Charles Thomas Cayce. "First, he envisioned, correctly, that the East Coast of the United States would become a major population center, from New England to Miami. The location on the coast between New York City and Washington in the north, and the large population of Florida in the south, would mean lots of traffic back and forth, and a tremendous increase in the population in this area itself that would be helpful to his work.

"The second reason was a kind of metaphysical condition. Virginia Beach was near two large bodies of water — the Chesapeake Bay and the Atlantic Ocean, and the sand of the beach had special energy in it. There was an implication about the energies of the area being particularly conducive to psychic forces. This would be helpful in his giving of readings, sort of like good transmission."

The Incredible Feats of "Old Crump"

(Author's note: During an interview with Charles Thomas Cayce for the preceding chapter, I gained leads for several other area ghost stories. In particular, Charles Thomas mentioned hearing his family talk of one of the most baffling and interesting episodes of strange psychic phenomena ever recorded in Tidewater; one that intrigued Edgar Cayce and both his sons, Hugh Lynn, and Edgar Evans. It also is one of the most durable cases of poltergeist-type activity on record. It began around the turn of the 20th century and continued for more than 40 years, and possibly longer.

Details on the story were extremely elusive. A number of people recalled hearing about the incidents, and a few remembered reading about them in yellowed newspaper clippings 50 to 75 years old. With the help of Mae Gimbert St. Clair, who works at the Association for Research and Enlightenment, and who witnessed some Edgar Cayce readings half a century ago, the search led to an old file cabinet, half-hidden in a corner at the A.R.E. library. There, in an obscure file titled "Poltergeist", which looked as if it hadn't been opened for years, was a treasure trove of information regarding a most fascinating tale. The following is thus pieced together from interviews, ancient news clippings, and a personal account from a family history.

The saga began one night in 1898 when young Henry Stone, who had recently been blinded in a hunting accident, came to spend the night with his friend, Eugene Burroughs at an old farmhouse in Sigma, near the present area of Pungo in Virginia Beach.

They were each about eight years old, and because the house was crowded with guests, the boys slept on a pallet on the parlor floor. Burroughs was roused when his pillow "slid away from under his head." He blamed Stone, who claimed innocence. Then Stone's pillow sailed across the floor, and they got into a fight which subsequently was broken up by Burroughs' father. When they told him what had happened, he laughed and said it was just the spirit of "Old Crump" — a man named Crump Bonney who had died in the house a century before. After Mr. Burroughs left, the boys said "things, like cats", kept walking across their feet, and chairs and other pieces of furniture seemed to "parade in a circle around the room." Frightened, but unharmed, they finally nodded off to sleep.

For the next 40-plus years, whenever Stone and Burroughs got together, an invisible force inexplicably moved objects about. And not just small objects. Pot-bellied stoves, bunk beds and chests of drawers slid across rooms, and in several instances, men and women were jostled about. "I cannot explain it," Burroughs said years later, "but that's the way it has been ever since Henry and I were boys." Such incidents were witnessed, documented and written about by scores of investigators, including doctors, scientists, newspaper reporters and lawyers. In fact, as time went on, and the story of the awesome phenomena got around, hundreds of people from all over the country came to see special seances Stone and Burroughs held, and they were rarely disappointed.

Two of the most expert witnesses were Edgar Cayce, the famous psychic, and his son, Hugh Lynn. Hugh Lynn sat in on a number of meetings with Stone and Burroughs and commented that the force was not very active when he was present. Once, however, a manifestation did occur that he could not explain. "It was pitch dark," he wrote later, "and I sat between Burroughs and Stone, with one foot on one of Stone's feet, and my hand and other foot on Burroughs. A picture came off the wall. I got up and put it back, winding the wire about the nail to make it more secure. Then I insisted that Burroughs and Stone stand in the middle of the room. Again, the picture came off the wall. This I can't explain."

As the boys grew older, the "happenings" grew stronger and more varied. Burroughs, for example, recorded the following in a privately published family chronicle: "We went to bed early; hardly had we put the light out and gotten into bed before our pillows left the bed and the covering followed. We decided to let the invisible force take everything it wanted and not try to get anything back, but the force threw everything back on the bed.

"Just then a big old-fashioned rocking chair hopped on the bed. It only felt as heavy as an ordinary chair when it first landed, but the longer it stayed the heavier it got. We thought it best to put it on the floor, and that is when the wrestle started. It took about 30 minutes to get out from under the chair. We held a little conference and decided to put the chair, pillows and covering out of the room, which we did, the pillows in a big wood chest in the hall and the chair near the chest. We came back and fastened the door with an old-fashioned night latch. We got back in bed and the pillows from the hall were already there! Again, before we had time to do any investigating, the chair was on the bed."

Crump, Burroughs said, made objects, heavy or light, even people, go sailing about, irrespective of gravity, thick walls "or the personal wishes of those present." Particularly disturbing events occurred during the winter of 1906. Burroughs' parents were away from home for a few days, so Henry and another boy, Joe Walters, came over to stay with him. The first night, they couldn't keep their pillows and covers on the beds, and the next morning Joe wanted to leave, but they persuaded him to stay. That night the pillows and blankets "acted up again," so the next evening they hatched a plan to "catch" the invisible force.

Remembered Burroughs: "After locking all windows and doors, we knew there was only one place where Crump could enter — through the stove pipe hole in the chimney. Henry agreed to sit by the chimney. When we were sure Crump was in the room, he was to put heavy cardboard over the hole. Then it would be up to Joe and me to catch Old Crump.

"Joe and I went to bed. It wasn't long before Henry yelled, 'He's got my hand!' Joe and I rushed to him, but he had been dragged under the bed! The cardboard had been torn in two. We were very frightened. We decided to keep the lamp burning and to sit up the rest of the night." That was enough for Walters. He went home.

Two nights later, with Stone and Boyd Beecham there to spend the evening, the manifestations continued. Said Burroughs: "After a half hour, our shoes fell heavily onto the bed. The covers crept away. I thought that Crump never worked in the light, and, since we were in no mood to go without blankets that night, we lit a lamp. I'd scarcely gotten into bed when the lamp flew over from the dresser, about 15 feet away, and nudged me. It was still burning. I returned it to the dresser and wearily crawled back into bed. The lamp sailed right back and was on us again.

"We got a lantern and a piece of rope from the barn, but now the lantern jumped onto the bed. I tied the lantern to the bedpost with the rope, whereupon the lantern began to rattle. 'You can jump as much as you please,' I told the lantern, 'but you can't get on the bed this time.' With that, the bed turned bottom up."

After that harrowing experience, Stone and Burroughs did not get together again for two years. In April 1908, they both were working for the Stephens and Easter Fish Company at their packing house in Virginia Beach. Dog-tired after a hard day's work, they both decided to spend the night in the company's bunk house. After all, Crump had only shown up in Burroughs' home. Burroughs shakenly recalled what happened next: "During the night a terrible crash shattered the quiet. The pipes of the kitchen cookstove at the far end of the house had fallen. The stove came sailing 25 feet in mid-air — to stop by our beds. I jumped out of the window and the stove crashed to the floor.

"The next night several fellows from the other camp saw shoes, clothing, fishing gear — everything, thrown onto the bunks — except the stove. After the men returned to their camp, we went to bed with the lantern lit. It landed on us still lighted. Harry Flanagan, the plant engineer, came by and suggested we tie the lantern. With us, he saw the lantern rattle and jerk from its lashing. It sat on us; then, after five minutes, flew back to the floor and sat. When the lantern came back to us, we grabbed it. The upper frame stayed in our hands, but the bottom section and chimney fell to the floor." At this point, Burroughs left to spend the rest of the night in another camp, and nothing else happened.

As the years passed, curiosity seekers came from all over, besieging the two men to make the mystery force appear. On one such occasion Burroughs' sister-in-law brought a group of women to the old farmhouse in Sigma. Burroughs told about it in the family publication. "The force seemed to take pleasure in entertaining everybody," he wrote. It inevitably began throwing pictures around the room, very much to the amusement of our guests. For awhile it had everybody excited. It changed from throwing pictures to pillows.

"Everybody began to relax. Just then we could hear a noise in the next room. In came an automatic shotgun loaded with five shells. When everybody found just what it was, we all came near fainting. We moved very carefully and took our time extracting the shells from the gun. The gun was put out of the room and then, as everybody was jabbering, Mr. Stone, Burroughs, and several others were thrown to the middle of the floor, their chairs on top of them.

"It was a scramble to try to get on your feet and place yourself where you were, seeing how easily the invisible force handled all those people. Fear began to come into the room and everyone was tense. Finally, they settled down again, but not for long. There came a crash and in came our coats. They had been put in the adjoining room on a bed. We decided it was time to go home, but a few stayed to see what else would happen.

"Soon a little noise was heard in the bedroom. Just then, in came a quilt, then came the mattress. Another loud crash —one that sounded as if the door was coming down between the living room and the bedroom. We investigated and found the bedstead jammed in the door leading to the living room. Everyone went home after that."

Through all the "visitations", Burroughs maintained that neither he nor Stone had any control over what might happen when they got together. He recalled one special incident which seemed to bear him out. "Once," he said, "Stone and I met unexpectedly on a street in Norfolk. Immediately, stones, bottles and other things began rolling toward us. We had to get off the street before we alarmed passersby."

But there was one unconfirmed story that suggested they could, on occasion, "will" the spirit. Charles Thomas Cayce said he heard that once one of the two, either Stone or Burroughs, owed some money to a country grocer in the Pungo area and they got in an argument over it. Cayce said that one day all the grocer's stock "moved" from the shelves to outside the store, bewildering the grocer. "It was never clear just how much control they had over the force, or if they had any control at all," Cayce noted. "Maybe the force just moved things at random."

One person who had first hand knowledge of "the Stone and Burroughs show" is Mrs. Thelma LaBarrer who still lives in Virginia Beach. She remembers a time when her late husband and a friend stayed with the two men one night, sitting on their bed to hold the covers on. The covers kept coming down anyway. She said things would come off the wall and fly around the room whenever Stone and Burroughs got together.

In 1925, Dr. J. Malcolm Byrd, from the prestigious Scientific American magazine came to Virginia to investigate the force. He told Burroughs that they should try communicating with the spirit by means of tapping. "The first time we tried to talk to Crump," Burroughs said, "was at 12:30 the night of July 5th, 1925. We went out to the barn so as not to disturb Mrs. Stone. After about five minutes in the inky blackness, Crump threw some sticks into my lap.

"I said, 'Invisible Force, I have been informed that you will talk to us. If so, speak.' No response. 'How about talking to you in code?' I said. 'One knock for yes, two knocks for no, three knocks for I don't know. If this is satisfactory, knock once.' We heard one really loud knock. My stomach contracted with fear. I had a thousand questions to ask him and all of them left me. I did manage to ask, 'Who are you?' He replied 'Uncle Billy.' He was my mother's uncle who I had known as a small boy and who died only a few years prior to the beginning of the poltergeist activity. We still called him Old Crump." Later, Burroughs added, they talked to the invisible force many times and he often replied, with the best results coming when the moon was full.

Dr. Boyd warned the men not ever to make the force mad. "You don't know what you're dealing with nor how much harm it may do you," he said. "We've never made the force mad as far as we know," Burroughs said. "No one was ever hurt by it — except a few who have hurt themselves in their haste to get away from a seance."

Burroughs said Old Crump could create all kinds of physical noises, including, for example, the "rip" of stitches being torn apart, or the grinding of a hole being bored through a wall, or even music from a piano. Once, when Burroughs' uncle came to Sigma for a visit, "a lot of toilet articles came into the room. He told his nephew that he bet nothing else would

203

move in the room when he propped himself against the door. "At that moment we heard a boring sound as of an auger boring a hole through the wall," Burroughs said. "Then a Coca-Cola bottle appeared in Uncle Jerome's hand. He marked it to identify it and put it in another part of the room. It returned to him as mysteriously as before."

Burroughs said some persons experienced a cold rush of air on their cheek, or the feeling of being rapped on their legs, or having ice put down their back. "Once a pillow in my hands began to breathe like a living thing! I beat on the pillow to make it stop, but it jumped out of my arms and slid across the room," he continued.

One of the most terrifying of all "force" experiences took place when Stone and Burroughs were talked into giving a special seance during a vaudeville-type show. They had stopped giving seances because they felt they could not control the spirit, but on this occasion they relented. The event drew headlines in the local paper, and so many people tried to wedge their way into Girkins Hall in Norfolk, that Stone and Burroughs had to have a police escort to get there.

The force apparently had temporary stagefright that night, because the men sat on the stage for nearly an hour and nothing happened. With the audience getting restless, Burroughs appealed to some of his spiritualist friends to see if they knew something that would "hurry things up." About 25 people joined hands and said a prayer.

Burroughs picks up the story from there. "In a few minutes, a young lady opposite me rose to her feet. She put her hands out and in a moment sailed over to me. She traveled a distance of 12 feet after swaying a moment there in her place. Fortunately, I was able to catch her. I gave her a hard push and let go. She stretched out in a horizontal position about two feet above the floor, her arms still straight in the air. She was lowered slowly to the floor during a period of about five minutes.

"I then tried to stand her up straight, but she was completely rigid. We called a doctor. He checked her and whispered in my ear, 'Burroughs, she's dead! She has no heart beat nor pulse.' I asked him how she could become rigid in so short a time. I was alarmed. A friend of mine, captain Ford, helped the doctor and me to stand her on her feet. She was so stiff

204

you could have broken her fingers like match sticks. The Randalls (professional magicians also performing that night) told me to tell her she was all right.

"I did that. I kept repeating it and after 10 minutes, she drew a long breath. She came to relax and we were able to sit her on a chair. I asked her to explain to the audience that she was not a part of the show and to tell us what had happened to her. She said she didn't remember anything after joining hands."

Burroughs said he, too, had been suspended in mid-air "many times." Other persons were transported about the room during such sittings. "I never had attributed this power to myself," Burroughs said, "but always to the Invisible Force. Certainly, I was not conscious of any will to transport myself or any one else."

Another time, Stone and Burroughs and two friends were approaching a barn when a corn planter, with no one in it, headed directly toward them. They stopped it and tried to take it back to the barn, but it "rolled out in the yard for some distance and fell over." Inside the barn a grass scythe, hanging on a wall, "came down from its hook on the wall" and fell across one of the men's laps. Burroughs also said that many times people tried to "trick" the force, or to catch it, never with any success, and often with unnerving results. One photographer who had brought his camera to take pictures one night was, according to Burroughs, "heaved, camera and all, out the door."

Throughout their lives, Henry Stone and Eugene Burroughs never really found out what caused the psychic invisible force. "I keep hoping I'll understand some day about the strange powers that Henry and I possess," Burroughs once said. "We have discovered that our sons also engender the Force when they meet. Is it inherited?" Indeed, the younger Burroughs said in 1968 that he "had witnessed the events brought about by his father's association with Stone, and that he himself also had been the victim of similar happenings when in the presence of Stone's son. It has been many years since anything has happened. We were young teenagers the last time the force manifested itself."

"Is the Force part of our subconscious minds?" the elder Burroughs once asked. "Is it mischievous spirits that enjoy our amazement at their pranks? Or is it really Uncle Billy Cox?"

Or is it "Old Crump?"

Whatever it was, it was very real. Said Hugh Lynn Cayce many years ago: "I have talked to many honest, intelligent people who certainly believe they heard and saw all manner of poltergeist activity. I cannot explain it."

CHAPTER 35

Is all that we see or seem

But a dream within a

dream?

(A Dream Within A Dream)

The Psychic Search for Chief Black Foot

(Author's note: After hearing of, reading about, listening to, and otherwise personally investigating literally hundreds of ghost stories over the past dozen years or so, there are times when I get the feeling that I have been doing this too long; that maybe I have heard it all. How many footsteps in the attic can one write about? But fortunately, each time this has happened, along comes an incredible tale that jolts the psyche and defies belief.

Such is the real-life saga of Victoria Mauricio, a Virginia Beach psychic-healer. I first learned of her through another psychic, a friend of mine, Kay Buchanan, who told me about a woman who found "the bones of a great Indian Chief". Her name was "Victoria something," Kay had said. I was intrigued. After some asking around, I found Mrs. Mauricio, now a widow in her sixties, who was gracious enough to grant me an extended interview.

She is, she told me, a psychic from a family of psychics which runs back 1,000 years! "I had a strange birth. It took a week. I was born with hair almost six feet long. Long, thin strands. Isn't that odd? And I weighed only two pounds," she says. She was born in South Wales. "For all my life I have been involved with psychic phenomena. My mother, grandmother and aunt were all psychic." She married an American after World War II, had a son, and moved to this country in 1952, eventually settling in Princess Anne County.

At a chapel in the area she heard that people had Indian guardian angels, but when she inquired as to whose hers was she was brusquely told that she didn't have one because she was not American. It was a slight she wouldn't forget. In time, she set up a psychic healing practice in Virginia Beach, at which she is still active to a select clientele.

What is doubly remarkable about the extraordinary experience she had, which began in 1975, climaxed in 1978, and continues today, is that it has been so well documented. When her story became known in 1978, NBC television filmed it; the former network program, "That's Incredible," did two segments on it; a local station did a "P.M. Magazine" piece for TV; Fate Magazine, the national publication on psychic phenomena, did a cover story; National Enquirer ran a large feature; and scores of other newspapers and radio stations, large and small, from Norfolk to Cody, Wyoming, and Billings, Montana, all covered it extensively. Wilford Kale, writing in the Richmond Times-Dispatch, called it an episode "straight out of the Twilight Zone". Victoria herself wrote a book on her adventures called "The Return of Chief Black Foot". It is a fascinating account which, unfortunately, is today out of print, although there is a copy at the Virginia Beach library.

And now, here is Victoria's story.)

It all began one night in September 1975, when she was asleep in her bed with her husband. She was suddenly awakened by the distinct — and loud — sound of drums beating. "And I can tell you this," she emphasizes today, years later, "it was not a dream. It was real." She awoke to find the bedroom ceiling and roof of her house had disappeared and she was staring straight up at a darkened sky pierced only by shafts of moonlight.

She tried to sit up, but then realized, to her horror, that she was buried in prairie dirt up to her neck. Blades of grass tickled her cheeks. As the drumming grew more intense, Victoria says, "a group of Indians in war paint came into view. They glared at me menacingly, then began to dance and chant. I was terrified." She was afraid she was about to be scalped. "I said to myself, let it be fast so I won't suffer," she recalls.

She tried desperately to scream, but no sound came from her throat. As her fears mounted, a huge Indian, standing six feet five inches tall and brandishing a large tomahawk, approached. He had coal black hair, braided and hanging nearly to his waist, and he was wearing buckskin pants and a breech cloth. At his appearance, the other Indians fell into an awed silence. He raised his hands to the sky and yelled, "Peace, brothers, not war." With that, the band of warriors quickly dispersed.

The great Indian then walked over to Victoria, who feared his tomahawk would soon be embedded in her head. Instead, he told her not to be afraid. "I am your Indian guide," he announced. "I am the spiritual one you have asked for. I am Black Foot of the Crow. I will protect you." He then pointed to his weapon and added, "This will be a sign between you and me. I shall be back to talk to you." He then disappeared, and Victoria felt no more fear. "Almost immediately I saw the room spin and there I was in my bedroom," she says.

This was the bizarre beginning of an unusual loving relationship that has lasted through the years and changed Victoria's life. Over the next several months Black Foot "visited" her regularly in her home in Virginia Beach. "I always saw him as you would see another person standing before you. He was just there, although I never knew how he came or went," she says. They often talked about psychic things, and Victoria had the feeling she was somehow being tested. Her attempts to question him as to why he was there were ignored.

In the spring of 1976 he came to her and said her patience had been good. He told her he wanted her to go to the "room of many books", which she interpreted as the library, and he said, "There, you will find a picture of me. Look in the book of the Plains Indians. I shall be holding a tomahawk." After hours of poring over books at the library, Victoria finally found a photo of five Crow Indians. Black Foot, clasping his tomahawk, was the second on the left.

The next day he appeared to her again and told her, "You must contact my people." When she asked him what she should say to them," he just smiled and then was gone again. "I sensed that his communication had more than ordinary significance," she later said. His cryptic comment led her on a zig-zagging chase to track down the Crow Indians. Eventually, she contacted a woman named Clara Turner, whose Indian name was Clara Whitehip. She worked for the Bureau of Indian Affairs on the Crow Reservation near Billings, Montana. When Victoria explained her mission — to find out about Black Foot — Clara told her she had never heard of him, but she would check with tribal historians.

Some time later Clara called back and told Victoria that Black Foot, indeed, had been a very famous Crow. He had been a chief of chiefs. She had not recognized the name earlier because the Crow had referred to him as "Chief Sits-in-the-Middle-of-the-Land". She sent Victoria a packet of information on the chief and the history of the Crows.

Over the next two years, Victoria continued to have encounters with the chief, but still there was no inkling as to what he wanted. In the meantime, she developed a friendship by long distance with the Crow people in Montana. When they learned that she was a psychic healer they began asking for her assistance. When one Indian disappeared from the reservation, some thought he was dead, but Victoria assured them he wasn't. She told them he was an epileptic and had left temporarily because he was angry over a family fight. (She

Victoria Mauricio

was right.) Another time a child was missing overnight and Victoria was called. Black Foot told her the child was dead, then, through Victoria, he gave details of where her body could be found, which also proved unerringly accurate.

Meanwhile, Black Foot began prodding Victoria to go to the Crow people in Montana. One evening while she was in a trance state, he said, "You are to go to the mountains as soon as possible. The time is right for you to go now." By this time Victoria's relationship with Clara and the Crow people had developed into a warm personal one, through the many telephone conversations they had, and through the long-distance healings.

And so, on July 11, 1978, Victoria and her friend from Virginia Beach, Barbara Neilson, boarded a plane and headed west. They were welcomed on the reservation as honored guests, were treated royally, and were showered with Indian gifts. On July 15, as Victoria prepared to go to a sun dance ceremony, Black Foot came to her and, at last, told her what he wanted. He said, "I want to be brought back to the reservation. I am in white man's land and I want to come home."

By now, after considerable research, Victoria knew a lot about Black Foot, and his message made sense to her. He was born about 1795 near or in the Absaroka Mountains of the western Big Horn Basin — a time when there were no white men present. He had grown up hunting the abundant buffalo, elk, mountain sheep, bear, deer, antelope, small game, birds and fish. He became a great Crow leader — a chief of chiefs — who headed the Indian representatives when the important Treaty of Fort Laramie was signed in 1868, which established the Crow reservation boundary and included a provision allowing Crows to hunt on unoccupied federal lands. It was Black Foot who decreed, ahead of his time, that all decisions of the tribe should be made by the majority and not just by the chiefs.

After the Crow reservation boundary was established by the Treaty of Fort Laramie, chief Black Foot said to his people: "So long as there is one living Crow Indian, he will have a place to come home to. The earth of the reservation is your mother . . . your second mother, and she will shelter and protect you . . ."

211

In 1877, when the majestic chief was in his eighties, he and his wife went off the reservation, in the direction of northern Wyoming, on a hunting trip. They are believed to have caught pneumonia and to have died within a day of each other. Their remains had never been found although the Crow had been searching for them for more than 100 years.

This is why, Victoria believed then, he had come to her. She was a psychic. Through her, Black Foot would lead the Crow to his burial grounds so that he could be taken from the "white man's land", and be reinterred among his own people.

"Now," said Victoria, "my mission was clear."

Soon after, the chief made it known that he wanted to speak to his people through Victoria. She was advised to hold a seance in the home of a Crow medicine man, or shaman. Arrangements were made for the seance at shaman Francis Stewart's house. There was to be only a small group attending, but word of the event had leaked out and when Victoria arrived, the house was jammed with Crows. Reluctantly, she proceeded. It was agreed that Black Foot's presence would be determined by the "swaying and flaring up" of a candle.

Victoria went into a trance. In a few minutes the candle swung violently from side to side, then flamed high in the air. When Black Foot made his presence known, Barbara Neilson said Victoria's face "took on the features of the chief. Her cheekbones got high and a blue streak appeared from her mouth down her neck." The chief told the audience that he wanted them to bring his remains back home, and then, speaking in Crow to the shaman, he said when that happened, his people would prosper.

Later, shaman Stewart cried. He told Victoria that this was the culmination of a prophecy made in Crow history more than a century earlier: that a great chief would be brought back and "miracle" healings would come from an outsider.

For the remainder of her stay in Montana, Victoria led a series of healing sessions, "and the cures were many." Before she left to come back to Virginia, she told historian Joe Medicine Crow that Black Foot had often said something like "Tse Tse." It had no meaning to her, but Joe was immediately shaken. He told her there was a town across the Wyoming border called Meeteetse. "That must be where he is buried," Joe exclaimed. Previously, the Crow had suspected Black Foot's remains were somewhere near Cody, Wyoming, about 75 miles to the west, halfway to the Yellowstone National Park.

The Crows were excited by this news and began to organize a search party. Just before Victoria left, Black Foot appeared to her and said, "Tell them to start the search. I will direct them through you to where I am." She then returned to Virginia Beach on July 25, 1978.

From that point on, the clues from the chief and the transmittal of them by phone from Victoria to the Crow in Montana came fast and furious. Over a period of the next four weeks she relayed the following signals:

- A pitchfork would somehow enter the picture.
- Seven white women would "appear" before they found the chief.
- There would be three odd-shaped rocks, and a tree "like a finger".
- The hooting of an owl would be heard in the daytime.
- The ground would glisten.
- An animal's scratching would be heard.

None of this made any sense to Victoria at the time, but she passed on the messages anyway. Several of the Crow went on the search on weekends in July and August. They were joined by Bob Edgar, a Cody historian and archeologist. It was tedious, exhausting work, but the party began drawing nearer to their quest. In an area near Meeteetse, above the Greybull River and 100 miles south of Billings, the clues seemed to be falling in place. They came upon the Pitchfork Ranch. It was owned by a woman who had seven heirs — all of them women. They heard an owl hooting — another key sign. They were getting closer. They called Victoria. She told them to go through a gate and look for the highest ridge. There would be three outstanding rocks and a big pine tree to the right of the opening of a cave. She said they would hear scratching sounds when they were near where the chief was lying, and that there would be a glitter when the sun hit the rock.

The search party found the rocks, the tree and the ridge precisely as described. The also heard scratching sounds, and, as darkness fell, there was another omen that hadn't been described. One of the Crow saw "what looked like a person" disappear behind a pine tree, move toward a rock, and then vanish! In the enveloping gloom, a flashlight beam hit a rock

and "the whole area was aglitter."

The team had to call it a night and return home, convinced they had located the general area of the sacred site. The last weekend in August they returned and climbed the ridge. Once again, as they did, Victoria was awakened in her home by Black Foot. He told her he would be found that day. High on the side of the ridge, above the Greybull River, 17-year-old searcher Willie Plainfeather entered a sandstone cave. Apprehensive, he looked around and then started to leave when a strange incident happened. He felt a "thing" grab his shoulder and then literally throw him into the interior of the cave. It is best told in Willie's own words: "I couldn't explain what it was," he said. "I went into the cave and had a funny feeling, as though someone was there with me. This scared me and I wanted to get out of there. When I turned to go I felt someone grab my shoulder and throw me in. All of a sudden I saw this bone, like it came up through the floor of the cave. It was the weirdest thing I ever saw. And then I saw the buffalo hide and a lot of other things so I went to get the others. As he did, he excitedly yelled, "I found it. I found It."

What they saw, near the east wall of the cave, was the end of a human arm bone protruding from the cave floor. There, half buried in the sand, was the skeleton of a very large man, surrounded by black, white and blue beads — all the trappings of a great chief laid to rest. Strangely, there were no signs of the chief's wife's bones.

Bob Edgar, the archeologist, said all the pieces of the puzzle fit Black Foot. The wear on the teeth, he noted, indicated an old man, and the length of the bones showed that he was very tall. Black Foot was six foot five and in his eighties when he died. The beads found with the remains were made before 1850, Edgar added. Another expert said the beads were of extremely valuable crystal "of a type worn only by Indian chiefs."

When Victoria was called with the news later in the day, before they told her, she said, "I know. You've found him!" After the remains were carried down from the cave, a special ceremony was performed. A blanket was laid out on the ground and the bones and beads were placed at one end. A braid of sweet grass was then lit, and the smoke was circulated around the bones. Everyone rubbed their skin with sage, to cleanse themselves for the ceremony. Then shaman Francis Stewart took out his long pipe, pointed it directly at the bones, and gave a long prayer in the Crow language. The pipe was lit and passed around the circle of searchers.

Chief Black Foot, again through Victoria, arranged his own "proper" funeral. He told her when he wanted to be buried — October 4th, 1978 — and where, close to the Bureau of Indian Affairs Office near the Crow Reservation. Victoria flew out for the event, which was a glorious affair attended by about 2,000 Crows and others including a host of television crews and newspeople. The story had been front page news throughout the West.

Victoria was invited to take part in a dance around the grave site. Then she was asked to speak. As she stood up to address the crowd, she saw Chief Black Foot, "standing by his coffin, in all his dignity. He nodded approval to me," she said. During her talk a large bald eagle flew overhead at treetop level, and when she ended her speech, the eagle screamed and flew off. "The Indian friends there were amazed to see this phenomenon," Victoria said. "To most of them, it was the ultimate proof that Chief Black Foot was there . . . A genuine psychic event had taken place. The great Chief was an eagle shaman and always worked with the birds, using their feathers. He wore the largest eagle feather in his hair and it was legendary."

A monument was built with the following inscription: "He that sits in the middle of the land. Chief of all chiefs of the Crow nation. Founder of the Constitution and the Crow Reservation . . ."

When most of the crowd had left, Victoria, alone, walked back to the grave site wondering now, at last, if the chief was satisfied. He appeared before her once again and nodded. Then he spoke. "Yes! he said. "Now I am with them (the Crow), and I can do the work that was unfinished when I died."

"I felt great satisfaction with his reply," Victoria Mauricio said.

The Crow gave her some of the beads that had been found with the chief's remains in the cave. She treasures them. They have also accepted her as one of their own, and have bestowed many honors upon her.

"You and my people are now one," Black Foot told her.

* * * * *

There is no rational explanation for the way she (Victoria) directed the searchers to the bones," Dr. Richard Fletcher, associate professor of sociology at Eastern Virginia Medical School in Norfolk, said later. Fascinated with the story, he had accompanied Victoria to Montana for the chief's funeral. "I have studied the whole case from beginning to end — from the predictions to the actual finding of the bones," he added. "It's almost unbelievable."

* * * * *

It seems somewhat anti-climactic to add footnotes to this incredible story, but there are two of a very curious and interesting nature. The first is an experience which happened to Victoria on her first visit to Montana in July 1978. It has not been recorded in the thousands of words written about Chief Black Foot's return in the media, but Victoria noted it in her book.

She was taking a bath one day when the chief appeared to her. "No one will ever hurt my woman," he said. She asked him who his woman was, and he told her *she* was. Later, she asked one of her Indian friends what this meant. "It means you were his wife," the friend said. "Why would this great chief go all those thousands of miles, also to a strange country, to seek her out unless she was his wife during his lifetime?"

Victoria said this answer seemed to open "a gate of awareness" for her . . . "It explained many things to me and I sat in a sea of memories . . . What do you do when you realize the spiritual love had been that of a physical nature? . . .

"I knew the tallness and gentle nature of this formidable man, how he liked to walk naked in the teepee, have his skin rubbed with scented oil, his chest so huge and his figure tapered to slim hips; how his giant hands had caressed my hair, and how he smiled on me lovingly; and how my face had reached just above his chest as he held me in a warm embrace. He never spoke harshly to me. We sat by the fire together and his love always protected me, as he protected me now."

* * * * *

The second strange occurrence came some time after the chief's remains had been found. Back in Virginia Beach, one of the area television stations wanted to film an interview with Victoria to fit into a segment of a syndicated program called "P. M. Magazine." She agreed, and arrangements were made to do the shooting in a friend's house. The crew — producer, interviewer, cameraman and technicians arrived and set up their equipment. Nothing worked. So they packed everything up and left, setting another date for the filming. This time they brought a lot of backup equipment, but again nothing happened.

Said producer Bob Field: "We went out two times. We got in there the first time and we couldn't get any picture, and we had problems with the recorder. It just wouldn't respond. We were not getting anything. We took it back to the shop, and the engineers started it up — no problem. We rescheduled and came back out, and again this time there wasn't any picture. It was spooky. The crew had used the machine at other times

217

between the first and second shootings. The third time we went out, we didn't use our own equipment. We borrowed some from the station. We plugged it in and had trouble with that."

At this point the totally frustrated producer told Victoria that she looked uncomfortable, which she wasn't, but he suggested that she go out in the kitchen and fix some coffee. She did. In the kitchen, the vision of Chief Black Foot appeared to her. He was very angry. "I won't allow you to do this filming," he told her. "Why not?" she asked. "I just won't allow it," he repeated. "But that's not fair," she retorted. "A lot of people have gone to a lot of trouble to do this. It could be a very good thing for your people and for me. Why don't you want us to film this?"

"Because," Black Foot ranted, "Yellow Hair is here!" "Who?" Victoria asked. "Yellow Hair, the evil one." "Do you mean General (George) Custer?" Victoria queried. "Yes!" Victoria was incredulous. She knew that Black Foot, the Crow, and other Indian tribes all hated Custer, and also that, oddly, the Custer Battlefield was less than 50 miles from the Crow reservation in Montana. But what on earth did Black Foot mean?

"Go tell the producer why this can't be done," Black Foot demanded. Victoria went back into the other room and told the producer that Black Foot was here and he wouldn't allow the filming to take place because "Custer" was present. She thought the producer would think she was nuts, but instead he got a puzzled look on his face and replied, "how did he know that?" Now Victoria was bewildered. "What do you mean?" she asked. The producer turned to one of the cameramen in the room and said, "He's a direct blood descendent of General Custer!" Victoria looked at the young man and was amazed. Not only was he related, but he looked exactly like Custer's pictures, yellow hair and all! And further, his name was Phillip Armstrong McCutchen. His middle name was even the same as that of his famous ancestor! "That's astounding," Victoria mumbled.

She went back to Black Foot and explained that this man wasn't really General Custer, but merely a descendent, and that he shouldn't stop the filming because of such a strange coincidence. Black Foot frowned, but then, reluctantly, gave his approval for the interview to take place. Victoria told the crew their equipment would now work, and when they tried it, it did. The filming then took place without further incident.

"It really happened," Field said. "It was all kind of weird."

About the Author

L. B. Taylor, Jr. is a native Virginian. He was born in Lynchburg and has a BS degree in Journalism from Florida State University. For 10 years he worked as a writer, editor and public information officer for NASA and NASA contractors at the Kennedy Space Center in Florida, covering every major space flight through the Apollo 11 first manned landing on the moon in July 1969. For six years he was editor and publications manager for Rockwell International in Los Angeles and in Pittsburgh. Taylor moved to Williamsburg in 1974 as public relations director of BASF Corporation's Fibers Division. He is the author of more than 300 national magazine articles and 26 non-fiction books.

His research for the book "Haunted Houses," published in 1983 by Simon and Shuster, stimulated his interest in area psychic phenomena and led to the writing of his regional trilogy: "The Ghosts of Williamsburg"; "The Ghosts of Richmond"; and "The Ghosts of Tidewater".

Personally autographed copies of "The Ghosts of Williamsburg" — 84 pages, illustrated, $5 and "The Ghosts of Richmond" — 172 pages, illustrated, $8, are available from L. B. Taylor, Jr., 248 Archers Mead, Williamsburg, VA 23185.